# MEMORIES OF A METIS SETTLEMENT

## EIGHTY YEARS OF EAST PRAIRIE METIS SETTLEMENT WITH FIRSTHAND MEMORIES: 1939 TO TODAY

CONSTANCE BRISSENDEN, EDITOR

©Copyright 2018 East Prairie Metis Settlement.

A co-publication of East Prairie Metis Settlement (EPMS) and Theytus Books.

Library and Archives Canada Cataloguing in Publication

Memories of a Metis settlement / edited by Constance Brissenden.

ISBN 978-1-926886-50-3 (softcover)

    1. Métis--Land tenure--Prairie Provinces--History. 2. Land settlement--Prairie Provinces--History. I. Brissenden, Constance, 1947-, editor

E99.M47M38 2018         971.004'97         C2018-902916-1

To reprint any portion of this book, other than limited amounts for educational use, contact: EPMS, P.O. Box 1289, High Prairie, Alberta T0G 1E0, Tel: 780 523 2594. Community Development Coordinator: Joan Haggerty.

www.theytus.com
Theytus Books, 154 En'owkin Trail, RR#2, Site 50, Comp 8, Penticton, BC, Canada V2A 6J7, Tel: 250-493-7181

Designer: Dean Pickup, Canada Book Design

 Canada

Printed in Canada by RRD, Edmonton, Alberta.

# CONTENTS

Introduction: From the Elders ........................................ 5
Map: Alberta's Metis Settlements .................................. 6
CHAPTER 1 The Metis Settlements of Alberta ............ 7
CHAPTER 2 The Making of a Settlement .................. 10
CHAPTER 3 Promises, Promises .................................. 16
CHAPTER 4 On the Road ............................................. 27
CHAPTER 5 Housing, Or the Lack of It ..................... 32
CHAPTER 6 Survival Strategies ................................... 36
CHAPTER 7 Nature All Around Us ............................ 45
CHAPTER 8 Building the First School ....................... 53
CHAPTER 9 More Memories of Settlement Life ...... 59
CHAPTER 10 Today and Tomorrow ........................... 72
CHAPTER 11 Elders of Today ...................................... 87
IN LOVING MEMORY ................................................. 99

## 2018 METIS MEMORIES

Robert L'Hirondelle ....................................................... 14
Dorothy Bellerose .......................................................... 22
Frederic Lawrence Sawan ............................................. 31
Dennis Andrews ............................................................. 33
Larry Big Charles ........................................................... 37
Marcel Auger .................................................................. 50
Solomon R. Auger ......................................................... 65
Eliza Big Charles ............................................................ 74

# DEDICATION

To the determined early settlers of East Prairie Metis Settlement (EPMS). To the Elders of today. To the young people who will be our leaders of tomorrow.

# ACKNOWLEDGEMENTS

Of special note: Metis is spelled without an accent following usage of the Metis Settlements General Council. The red Metis flag (cover) is used by the Metis Settlements General Council.

Thank you to the Elders' Planning Committee (2018): Dennis Andrews, Marcel Auger, Dorothy Bellerose, George Bellerose, Eliza Big Charles, Murielle L'Hirondelle, Richard Patenaude, and Mildred Supernault. Thank you to all additional contributors, including Larry Big Charles, Myrna Dumont, Joan Haggerty, Robert L'Hirondelle, Frederic Lawrence Sawan, and Brian Supernault.

Thank you to editor/publication coordinator Constance Brissenden, www.firstnationswriter.com. Her partner, Cree author Larry Loyie (1933-2016), introduced her to the beauty of EPMS in the mid-1990s.

Thank you to the Metis Settlements General Council staff for their invaluable assistance, and to Josh Moran, Michif Cultural Connections, St. Albert, AB, for additional research.

**Cover Photos** Top left: Dorothy and George Bellerose; top right: Brian Supernault (white shirt), Jacob Howse. Bottom left: Maria Auger and her brother Joseph Auger holding nieces; bottom right: Elsie Sawan. All photos courtesy of the families.

# FROM THE ELDERS

*Memories of a Metis Settlement: Eighty Years of East Prairie Metis Settlement* shares memories of today's Elders and members.

It includes firsthand accounts of the settlers, first published as *East Prairie Metis, 1939 to 1979, Forty Years of Determination*. This edition is out of print and most of these heroic early settlers have passed on. We have included their memories so they will never be forgotten. Thank you to the original publishing team in 1979: project manager Carol Supernault, researchers Mary Auger and Marcella Cunningham, and typist/transcriber Velma Bellerose.

In *Memories of a Metis Settlement: Eighty Years of East Prairie Metis Settlement*, we have tried to capture the heart and soul of eighty years of East Prairie's Metis people.

Some of the Elders and contributors to the book in the EPMS community hall, March 2018. Left to right: Solomon R. Auger, Eliza Big Charles, Murielle L'Hirondelle, Dorothy Bellerose, George Bellerose, Marcel Auger. Front: Anne Marie Auger. Photo courtesy of Constance Brissenden.

# ALBERTA'S METIS SETTLEMENTS

Plans were originally made for twelve Metis settlements in Alberta. Eight still exist: Paddle Prairie, East Prairie, Peavine, Kikino, Gift Lake, Buffalo Lake, Elizabeth, and Fishing Lake.

Four additional settlements were dissolved in the 1950s: Touchwood, Marlboro, Cold Lake, and Wolf Lake.

Metis Settlements in Alberta are unique and vibrant communities. Together, they have a land base of 1.25 million acres. The communities are home to approximately 6,500 people, one-tenth of Alberta's total Metis population.

East Prairie Metis Settlement (EPMS) covers 32,635 hectares (334.44 km squared or 129.13 square miles). Membership is more than 900 people. EPMS (Range Road 161) is 35 km south of Highway 2 and the Hamlet of Enilda. The nearest town is High Prairie, 42 km to the northwest. Edmonton, the capital city of Alberta, is 394 km to the south.

Map courtesy Metis Settlements General Council.

— CHAPTER 1 —

# THE METIS SETTLEMENTS OF ALBERTA

Metis are one of the three distinct Aboriginal peoples of Canada recognized in section 35 of the *Constitution Act, 1982*, along with First Nations and Inuit.

The eight Metis settlements of Alberta are unique in Canada. They provide a land base for Metis people to live, work, and practise their Aboriginal right to hunt, fish, trap, and gather food, for ceremonial and medicinal purposes.

Metis people are the descendants of unions between European traders and Indigenous women. They once travelled widely across the Prairie Provinces of Canada and the Upper Midwest of the United States to trade, hunt, trap, and gather food. In the 19th century, Metis formed communities across what was then known as Rupert's Land, Northwest Territories, and Manitoba.

Leaders of the Provincial Executive Committee, Metis Association of Alberta, 1935. Back, left to right: Peter Tompkins, Felix Calihoo. Front, left to right: Malcolm Norris, Joseph Dion, James Brady. Artwork courtesy Metis Settlements General Council.

The creation of the Metis land base in Alberta was a long struggle. In 1928, Metis people in Alberta began to organize to protect their interests. In 1932, they met in St. Albert and formed the Metis Association of Alberta.

The first leaders of the Metis Association of Alberta were Joseph Dion, Felix Calihoo, Malcolm Norris, Jim Brady, and Peter Tompkins. Along with many, they worked diligently to benefit the Metis people of Alberta, and for no money – money was scarce. As one old-timer remembered, no one ever got paid, no matter what type of work they did.

### FORMING THE SETTLEMENTS

Metis fought hard and were determined to get land from the Canadian government. In 1938, Alberta passed the Metis Development Act, setting aside colonies (later known as settlements) for Metis people. Alberta was the first province in Canada to enact legislation specific to Metis.

Paddle Prairie was the first Metis colony to open. From then on, seven other colonies successfully opened up, Peavine, East Prairie, Kikino, Gift Lake, Buffalo Lake, Elizabeth, and Fishing Lake, all in Northern Alberta.

The Metis Development Branch, of Alberta's Social Services and Community Health, was set up to administer the affairs of the settlements once they were established.

— CHAPTER 2 —

# THE MAKING OF A SETTLEMENT

In 1939, East Prairie became a settlement. The Charlie Bellerose family and a bachelor, George Harvey, were already living on the land. They were followed by the Solomon Auger family. The next to move in were the L'Hirondelles, then Norbert Andrews. They were followed by Solomon Johnston.

The first council member was Charlie Bellerose.

Metis Peter Tompkins was the first supervisor, hired by the Metis Development Branch to act as a general manager for the community. The third supervisor was Jack Kachuk, who came from Hairy Hill, a farming community north of Vegreville, Alberta. Although not a trained educator, Jack was the first teacher in East Prairie.

Most of the settlers made their living by farming, trapping, doing odd jobs, and later on, by logging timber. For food, meat came from moose and deer, and vegetables from their gardens.

Housing at the beginning included tents, then log cabins with sod roofs, with little or no flooring. A few people had

Agatha and Louie Savard's first house was built in 1956 of old lumber from bunk shacks that had been thrown away by an old lumber camp. Photo from *East Prairie Metis, 1939-1979*.

lumber shacks. Standard-built houses did not come until 1959.

Transportation, at that time, was mainly by teams of horses and wagon. The road was always in terrible condition and got worse when it rained. The East Prairie River didn't help either. At every rainstorm, it flooded – and had to be crossed twice without the aid of a bridge.

Later, in 1945, a standard bridge was built with cables and logs. When the first flood came along, it was destroyed. Years later, in 1956, a footbridge was constructed, also held by cables. This was built high enough so that it didn't collapse when the river flooded. Six years later, another attempt was made at building a standard bridge. When it was completed, it too was demolished by a flood. After this, the footbridge continued to be used until the steel bridge was built in 1967.

## THE MANY ROLES OF WOMEN

Women were equal to men in their contributions to life in the settlement. They were mothers; they cooked; they cleaned; they made clothing for their children; they were gardeners. They endured hardships year-round.

Marguerite L'Hirondelle arrived in May 1942. Her husband, Maurice L'Hirondelle, and his father, Peter L'Hirondelle, heard about the East Prairie Colony and left from Lac La Nonne, Alberta, on August 15, 1941. They went over the Swan Hills with their cattle. Marguerite wished that Maurice had waited, for their daughter Elaine was born on September 7. Marguerite stayed behind with her young son and daughter, her mother and three sisters. Maurice had taken Frankie, another son, along with him.

Maurice wrote in February 1942 saying that their house was nearly ready to move in. On the way to East Prairie, Marguerite rode a big lumber wagon. She said later it would have been better walking in a foot of water than riding the bumpy wagon all day. On the way, they stopped at Haggerty Flats for dinner. Marguerite was too tired and discouraged to eat. Finally, she made it, but when she arrived, the house was not ready. She found that her husband had accidentally cut his leg while hurrying to finish it.

Maurice and Marguerite lived with his father for a while. As soon as possible, they moved into a tent. Finally, their first house was ready. "We were glad to move in," recalled Marguerite. "The fleas were not so bad in there. They were very bad in the tent."

Maurice and Marguerite L'Hirondelle had 14 children in all.

Maurice L'Hirondelle reunited with wife Marguerite and their children in 1942 in Lac La Nonne, AB, before taking them to live in the East Prairie Metis Colony. Photo from *East Prairie Metis, 1939-1979*.

---

"When I married Maurice L'Hirondelle on May 1, 1935, I didn't know he was already married to the Metis Association. He was the Secretary for the Lac La Nonne local. My dad, Samuel Majeau, was the President. Mr. George Savard and Mr. Peter L'Hirondelle were on the board. When there was a meeting, Maurice was sure to be there."

– Marguerite L'Hirondelle

---

## Robert L'Hirondelle: A Move for Women's Rights

I wasn't born yet when my father Roy and one of my uncles came to the settlement to visit my grandparents, Peter and Sophie, in 1940, but I remember my father telling me in later years that when he was with my uncle, my grandfather Peter asked them come to a meeting at East Prairie Colony.

Peter Tompkins was the supervisor at the time. When they were at the meeting, he told the people that if they didn't get more members to move to East Prairie, the settlement would be abolished. This had happened to four settlements, Touchwood, Wolf Lake, Cold Lake, and Marlboro. My father and uncle signed up for their membership so that the government could not take our Metis land away.

Another milestone was reached in 1982 for East Prairie Metis Settlement. This time, it involved land, membership, and voting. The way the membership worked was that a woman could not vote unless her husband was a member. Women could also not hold land.

A land issue came to the council that year regarding how much land a member could hold. My questions were: Why can't women have their own membership; why can't they hold their own land? It hadn't been done, but why not? Are men the only Metis in the settlement? I didn't think so.

The first woman who applied for membership, I believe, was either Darlene Bellerose or Yvonne L'Hirondelle. When they applied and were approved for membership, everything seemed to fall into place. They applied for land and received it.

As they say, the rest is history. The issue had never come up before regarding women's rights. I guess everyone thought that the rules for being a voting member and holding land were set in stone. We learned that rules could change, for the better. History is sometimes forgotten, especially if things just fall into place afterwards, with no fuss or bother. This change is worth noting and remembering.

The Metis women worked alongside their husbands. This is a fact. In 1982, they were recognized as members in their own right. They could hold land on their own.

— CHAPTER 3 —

# PROMISES, PROMISES

In the late 1930s, before the settlement was established, the Charlie Bellerose family and a bachelor named George Harvey lived in East Prairie. Solomon and Lucille Auger arrived in 1941.

Charlie Bellerose had worked around St. Albert and Edmonton, finally homesteading in Cork, Alberta, a small district near St. Paul. He married Bernadette Laboucan, on May 2, 1916. They had 13 children, four girls and nine boys. John Bellerose was the oldest. Charlie Bellerose farmed, raised pigs, chickens, and turkeys and had horses in the Cork area.

Son John Bellerose remembered, "Just when everything was looking good, and the prices of grain were going up, our dad received a letter from his sister, Justine Beaudry. She told him, 'Charlie there is a nice farming area called East Prairie. Nice soil, no rocks, a nice river, no taxes to pay. Why not move over here? We will help you out when you get here.'"

In 1938, Charlie and Bernadette Bellerose prepared to move. Charlie sold all the things he could sell. In those days no one had more money than the other so he didn't get too much for whatever he sold.

The family travelled by a team of horses and wagon loaded with their belongings: a few pieces of furniture, walking plow, tractor, disk, and harrows. It was a long trip and the hardships they endured were multitude, including mosquitoes, rain, and wagon breakdowns. They first stayed in Grouard, then around 1939 or 1940, they moved to East Prairie. John Bellerose remembers that it was a long, cold spring, with a snowstorm on Easter Sunday. At the end of April and in the first part of May, his folks took up residence at the Baker home. John gave the money he made – 35 dollars a month working for a Mr. Marquette all summer – to support his parents in East Prairie.

The wedding of Charlie Bellerose and Bernadette Laboucan, May 2, 1916. Photo from *East Prairie Metis, 1939-1979*.

## ONE FAMILY'S MOVE

Margaret Supernault, daughter of Solomon and Lucille Auger, recalled that they heard of the colonies (now known as settlements) opening up in 1939. Supervisor Peter Tompkins was trying to get the northern colonies (East Prairie, Paddle Prairie, Gift Lake, and Peavine) established. At the time, the Augers had a small farm in Salt Prairie, north of Grouard.

> **RECIPE**
>
> ### Bachelor Bannock
>
> *Early settler and bachelor George Harvey was a veteran of the First World War. He lost an eye in the war, had a glass eye, and was wounded in other parts of his body. After the war, George Harvey had a war disability pension. He helped others when they were in need. In return, they looked out for him.*
>
> Preheat oven to 350°F (177°C). In one mixing bowl, combine 3 cups flour, 1 tablespoon baking powder, 1 teaspoon salt, 1 teaspoon sugar. In another bowl, mix ½ cup milk and ½ cup water and beat in the egg. Pour the liquid into the bowl of dry ingredients and mix. Add water until it looks like cake dough, and then pour it into a greased pan. Bake about one-half to one hour, depending on the thickness of dough. *From Theresa Auger*

Solomon Auger wanted to move to East Prairie because they were promised everything: land, free housing, and more. Figuring that this golden opportunity shouldn't be passed up, the family decided to move. This was just after the Great Depression of the 1930s, so everything and anything sounded good.

Solomon and Lucille Auger arrived in July 1941. It took about four days to get to East Prairie in their old wagon. It kept breaking down, and the condition of the wagon roads didn't help matters. The cayuses, low-quality horses, kept getting stuck in the mud which also slowed the family down.

Finally on the third or fourth evening, the Augers made it to what is known as Bakers Crossing. It was raining and everyone was soaked. The Charlie Bellerose family was there to meet them. Young Margaret Auger (later Supernault) thought she had never seen so many kids in her life.

The Belleroses had a wagon, and they helped the Augers cross the river. They took the new arrivals to their home and gave them dry clothing, fed them, and bedded them down for the night. The Augers stayed at the Bellerose home for some time, as they really didn't have anywhere to live. Finally they left the Bellerose home to try to find a place of their own.

They came to George Harvey's place but they couldn't move in. George Harvey had been in Big Prairie all summer and the Augers didn't want to just barge in. They had an old tent that seemed to have a million holes in it, but they lived in the tent by the river anyway. All summer, it rained, with thunder and lightning. Mrs. Auger would light candles at night. Margaret, her daughter, wasn't sure why

Original settlers Lucille (Lucy) Auger and her brother Norbert Andrews at a Metis Association Assembly in Athabasca, in August of 1967. Lucy's daughter, Margaret Supernault, with some of her children in front of her log home in 1960. Photos from *East Prairie Metis, 1939-1979*.

she did this, but she thinks it was to protect the family from the thunder and lightning.

One good thing about the first East Prairie summer was that Solomon Auger was a good hunter, and provided his family with moose, deer, and bear meat. Edgar Bellerose would go hunting with him. When they killed something, they split the meat between the two families, the only families in East Prairie at the time. Bernadette Bellerose also had a big garden. Between the meat and the vegetables, they ate pretty well.

But all the things that had been promised to the Augers just weren't there. No lumber, nothing. Supervisor Peter Tompkins was sure the materials they had asked for had been shipped out to them, but no one knew where their order went.

---

**RECIPE**

### Sweet and Sour Moose Ribs

| | |
|---|---|
| 4 lbs moose ribs or brisket pieces | Salt and pepper |
| 4 cups water | 4 tablespoons soya sauce |
| 1 cup vinegar | Amount desired of rice (cook |
| 1 cup brown sugar | separately) |
| 1 can tomato soup | Cornstarch to thicken |

Cook the moose meat or brisket pieces for at least one hour in the four cups of water. Simmer for half an hour, adding vinegar, brown sugar, and tomato soup. Salt and pepper to taste. Add the soya sauce. Thicken with cornstarch. Serve hot with rice. The dish is served hot because the fat moose ribs tend to freeze in your mouth. This recipe combines the best of two worlds, the Metis and the Chinese.
*From Margaret Supernault*

Eventually, the Augers moved into a log house abandoned by Peter Tompkins. The house had a mud roof, bare ground floor, and no windows. When it rained, it rained right through the roof. Finally, Solomon Auger cut up some small logs, split them in half, and from these he made flooring.

## YOUNG PEOPLE WORKED HARD

In the early years of the settlement, young people worked hard. Felix Bellerose describes his first experience with farming, at the age of 12. His family had moved to East Prairie from Grouard in 1940, when Felix was nine.

Felix remembered: "In 1943, my dad and my brother farmed in East Prairie with four head of cayuses and a walking plow. That's the first time we had a crop out there.

Early settler Charlie Bellerose (centre left) and his sons, with visitor Leo Johnston standing at the extreme left, in the summer of 1942. Charlie and Bernadette Bellerose had 14 children. Photo from *East Prairie Metis, 1939-1979*.

When the land was ready to seed, we had no drill, so my dad and brother broadcast the seeds by hand. We used a disc to disc grain into the ground, harrowing it later. Then, in 1945, my dad bought a thrashing machine. We had to cut the bands of the grain to thrash it, feeding the machine by hand. That's the way we did it when we first started farming in East Prairie."

# Dorothy Bellerose: A Long Stretch of Road

I was born in Atikameg (aka Whitefish Lake), Alberta. My parents were Antoine (Tony) and Louisa Laboucan. When I was 18 years old, I married George Bellerose. George's birthday is on Valentine's Day. In 2018, he turned ninety and enjoyed a big party.

Before I came to East Prairie, I used to see this long stretch of road. I often wondered what was up there. I saw people coming out of there on horseback or a wagon team. That was before I met George. I wondered how far the road went, and then, the following year, I ended up there. I didn't know that I would be one of them coming in and out of that road, and never thought that I would end up there. But I didn't mind.

I came to East Prairie with George in the summer of 1957. When we came here, we caught a ride with someone. At first, we lived with George's sister, Helen, and her husband, Roy Haggerty. The Haggertys had a small log house. Their nearest neighbour was Henry Prince. At that time, people lived quite a ways from each other.

I remember that Helen Haggerty used to pick berries. She would go by herself. I thought that she was a brave woman, and I didn't go with her because I was scared of bears. They also had cows and she used to milk them. There was no power out there at the time. The only way she could keep the milk fresh was by putting it in a pail and lowering it down a well with a rope.

Traditional elders Philemine (Willier) and Alex Laboucan, Dorothy Bellerose's grandparents, in Whitefish Lake, around 1950. Photo courtesy Dorothy Bellerose.

We stayed with them for a few months. Then we moved in with Bernadette, George's mother, quite a distance from the Haggertys. She was the widow of Charlie Bellerose who passed away in 1953.

A lot of things have changed since the 1950s. What I notice most about the changes are the creeks and river. When I first came out here, I used to wash our clothes with a washboard. I would haul water from the river. The kids would go swimming. Nowadays the water is not drinkable; it's dried out and polluted. That's the water we used to drink and now we can't drink it.

When I was young, I went with my auntie to snare rabbits. Now I hardly ever see them. I notice that there are not as many birds, ducks, or geese. They seem scarce now.

The berries used to be all over. We were able to pick berries towards the McKinley area. Now there are no blueberries around. I mostly enjoy picking Saskatoon berries north of here in Big Prairie because it's a wide open space. You can see wild animals coming from quite far away. In the 1980s, we had a truck and camper. Sometimes we would camp when we were picking berries. We really enjoyed that.

Everybody had large gardens, growing cabbages and turnips, but these two won't grow anymore. Carrots still grow well, and all the other vegetables, except these two.

We had chickens and cows as the kids were growing up. We had horses and pigs for a few years. We had fresh eggs. Life wasn't bad; we were happier in those days because we'd visit our neighbours. Now we don't have time to visit because life is too busy. In those days, whoever killed a moose shared the meat; people seemed to get along better than they do now.

When I first came out here, the road was bad. The only way to get through was with a team of horses and a wagon. Sometimes the team would get stuck. There were a lot of mud holes and some were really deep.

Dorothy Bellerose in 1957, with horses and sleigh, soon after arriving in East Prairie. The horses' names were Beauty (left) and Kit. In the background is the house she and husband George lived in for a few months. Photo courtesy Dorothy Bellerose.

When the river flooded, the trees would go floating. During a flood, the trees would bust up the bridges. Finally, a bridge was built high enough so the trees would not reach it and destroy it. There was also a walking bridge. When we walked on it, we would bounce. It was scary because it felt like it was going to turn over… you would get dizzy.

A gravel road was built in the 1960s. School buses started taking the kids to High Prairie. I never thought I would ever see a paved road coming out to East Prairie, but it came along around 2006.

They put up the power lines when the gravel roads were built. That's when we got power to our houses. The telephone came along, with what was called party lines. I remember one of the neighbours was listening on the party line to these two people talking. One guy asked the other guy about something. He didn't know the answer, so he said, "Why don't you ask the third party?"

Back in the day, we used to have only one channel on our television which operated by a car battery.

Better houses started being built for community members in the 1960s. We also started having better vehicles because of better roads. I miss the horses, though, because I used to ride when I was with my parents. I would ride without a saddle sometimes.

I was never bored out here in East Prairie. I've lived here for more than sixty years now. After all my kids were grown up, about 1977, I worked as an instructor for East Prairie Wood Products for three years. I did carpentry off and on as the years went by, helping with the housing program. My son, Glen, was an apprentice carpenter and I worked with him. I also drove a bus for Alberta Vocational College for about seven years. I worked until I was about 68 years old.

George worked for the Alberta Department of Highways, and then started working for Alberta Forestry. When we worked in East Prairie for the settlement, we would be paid with vouchers for groceries instead of money. I was happy when he started working for Alberta Highways and Alberta Forestry. Then he was paid with a cheque.

I have no complaints about my time in East Prairie because I came to love this place. We never went hungry. Even though some people said it was hard, to me it wasn't.

Some of my kids don't live around here now, and I miss them. They are still my babies. I have grandchildren and great-grandchildren. They are all precious to me. They are the jewels in my heart. I've always wondered how I made it, raising eleven kids, but I know that by the grace of God I did it. He was with me the whole time and I thank Him for that.

A modern Metis wedding: Dorothy Bellerose (bottom row, left) and George Bellerose (second from right) gather with their children and grandchildren at the wedding of youngest daughter Sheila to Leroy Breast, July 26, 2008. Photo courtesy Dorothy Bellerose.

CHAPTER 4

# ON THE ROAD

Early families had dog teams, and horses and a wagon. They also walked, and rode horses. Sleighs were used in winter. Until the late 1960s, getting from one place to another was always difficult. Today, a paved road into the settlement and transportation of all types makes life easier.

### A MEAN LITTLE RIVER

Maurice L'Hirondelle, an early settler, recalled that travel was difficult in the early decades of the settlement: "There is a mean little river we call East Prairie River. Long ago, it used to flood any time. Roads were terrible, especially because of the river. We had to cross that river twice, wading our teams across. Sometimes when you left for your shopping trip, the river would be shallow and easy to cross, but while you were in town it rained hard. By the time you returned, you'd be able to cross the first crossing, but when you got to the second, it would already be halfway up the bank. You wouldn't be able to get across. This happened to many people. The people would have to make camp right there and wait for the river to go down. Sometimes before the river went down, they'd run out of food, and would have

Eddie L'Hirondelle, in 1950, pausing by his car on the newly completed bridge across the East Prairie River. The next year, a flood took out the bridge. Photo from *East Prairie Metis, 1939-1979*.

to go back to Enilda and get more food before they could go home. And if other people were on the other side of the river who had asked them to get groceries, they'd get pretty hungry, on account of not being able to get the food across. This didn't happen very often, but it happened sometimes."

Eddie L'Hirondelle also remembered the bad road conditions of the early years: "When we came to East Prairie to apply for land, there were only horses. Then, when the cars came out, there were only two cars out here. I had a car, and my son Gary had a car. The only time you could use a vehicle was when it was dry. In a rainstorm, we used horses. When it froze in the fall, we used the cars, although at that time there was no such thing as snowplowing around here."

## THE FIRST SUSPENSION BRIDGE

Around 1950, the settlers build the first suspension bridge in East Prairie. It was cable: there were four or five cables. Maurice L'Hirondelle remembered, "I think it was three strands of cable on each side, with the pier in the middle. We didn't build it high enough; we built on the first bank. After using it for about one year, the first high water came along. Down went the bridge with the driftwood. There again, we had no more bridge. I think it cost us around $5,000 including the material put into it. But we did get paid, I think 25 cents an hour, for building that bridge."

The settlers had wanted a steel bridge from the beginning. Now they were told by supervisor Jack Kachuk that the settlement was broke. It would have cost $10,000 to build a steel bridge. Looking back, the settlers were still shaking their heads that it cost $5,000, half of that, to build the first suspension bridge that was washed away.

The next bridge was started farther up the river. The supervisor, John Lovoie, thought he had a good plan. The government also thought it would work. The settlers got two sides built up with timber, set in the ground. Then John Lovoie left before finishing the second bridge, and another supervisor came in.

## SHOPPING...1940S STYLE

In the 1940s, the settlers did their shopping in Enilda. They bought staples such as sugar, flour, tea, salt, and tobacco. Because the roads were often bad, it took anywhere from one day to four days to get there, although it is only 35 km away.

Near Enilda, there was a place where they could camp across the tracks at an opening by the willows. Firewood was available, and grass for horses to feed on. When families went shopping together, there were sometimes four or five tents at the campground. Families would set up their tents when they got there and camp for the night. The next morning they did their shopping. After they had everything they needed, they would load up and haul their stuff home. Sometimes they got parts for machinery, if something had broken down, such as a much-used mower, rake, or plow. They would make the repairs when they were back home.

The first modern transportation was a Jeep owned by supervisor Zane Dedeluk. When settlers travelled to town for groceries in the Jeep, they would be back the same day. It was a big change from travelling for days to and from Enilda or High Prairie.

Horses and wagon, like this one, with settlers on the way to shop in Enilda, were used to move families into the settlement. The Greg Sawan family arrived in 1961. On the wagon, left to right: June (Zunie) Johnston, "Old" Peter L'Hirondelle, Peter's daughter Amelia Andrews.
Photo from *East Prairie Metis, 1939-1979*.

**2018 METIS MEMORIES**

*Moving in the early 1960s was as tough as ever. Compare the memories of father and son Greg and Frederic Lawrence Sawan.*

## Greg Sawan, Father:

❝ I first came to East Prairie in June 1961. I moved from Whitefish Lake (Atikameg), which is about 74 miles (120 km) from here. We moved with a team of horses and a wagon, because the roads were so bad. There were eight of us in all; my wife and me, and our six children. I left my family at Grouard and made the remainder of the trip alone. I came to pick some land for us to reside on. I did some odd jobs within the colony for the two months I was over here alone, living out in a tent. Then I went for my family. We lived an additional two months in that tent. After I finished putting up our log cabin, we moved in. We lived in that for one year." From *East Prairie Metis, 1939-1979, 40 Years of Determination.*

## Frederic Lawrence Sawan, Son:

❝ I was born in Atikameg. I remember travelling to East Prairie in 1961 by wagon. One memory stands out about our journey here, which is that the trail was so awful. The horses were getting stuck. We were told to get off the wagon so that the horses would have an easier time pulling it. The next memory is when my dad started to build a log house, so that we would have a place to live. I mixed straw with mud, which was used to fill in the cracks between the logs." — *In 2018*

— CHAPTER 5 —

# HOUSING, OR THE LACK OF IT

For many decades, where to live presented a problem. The transition was slow: from tent to sod-roof shack to log house to standard house to today's modern house.

### FAMILIES TOUGHED IT OUT

Solomon and Lucille Auger arrived soon after the colony opened. They ended up living in an old log house that looked like a barn. It had no flooring, but Solomon cut up small trees and from these made a floor. Sometimes the Auger daughters would ask each other to wash the floor, as the place around the cellar was pretty well-worn. "The house never looked quite clean – you know how a barn is – and the windows looked so small," one of the daughters recalled later.

The Augers next lived in an old, run-down shack from 1950 to 1967. The roof would leak so they changed the roof. The floor would cave in, so they changed that too. Finally the whole shack went down in one corner, so they moved out. Then in 1968, they had their new standard-built house.

The Greg and Elsie Sawan family arrived in 1962. They first lived in a tent, then for a year in a log house they built. For three years they lived in a house of lumber, built with help from their children. In 1967, they left the colony and moved into High Prairie because Mrs. Sawan was sick and they wanted to be near a doctor. After 11 years in town, renting from place to place, they moved back to East Prairie, because it was getting too expensive to live in town.

Food was still hard to come by. Greg Sawan remembered, "We lived mostly on moose meat and potatoes. I always use to put in a garden of potatoes, and I hunted a lot, because there was always plenty of moose then. I also did some trapping to help with our living expenses. My wife always canned a bunch of berries."

Dennis Andrews' family was one of the first to arrive. He is one of the oldest Elders living at EPMS. In 2018, he took time to write his childhood memories.

**2018 METIS MEMORIES**

## Dennis Andrews: Floating Down the River

I cannot give the year that we were arrived here, but I think it was before the East Prairie Metis Colony was opened up.

There was a white trapper and his wife by the name of Fitzsimmons. They lived past McKinley Creek in a sod-roof shack. George Harvey, a bachelor, lived where Gabe L'Hirondelle lives now. We also lived at the sod-roof shack past McKinley Creek by the river.

I wasn't very old then. I remember my older brother, Riel Andrews, and I were walking across the East Prairie River which was shallow at that time. I dropped one of my shoes and it started floating down the river. Riel went and grabbed my shoe, which was good because it was the only pair I had.

We also lived in those log cabins in the back of where Roy L'Hirondelle lived. I remember when the Bellerose family showed up. Us kids, we used to have fun playing around there. The settlement must have opened up by then.

My mother was determined that her children go to school. Pete Tompkins told my folks, 'There is going to be a school at Gift Lake.' So my mother and dad moved over there. By wagon, of course. I hated wagon rides. Too rough! We stayed at Gift Lake for four years, even though there was no school there either. My mom and dad moved back to East Prairie where I finally went to school when I was 12 years old. I quit school when I turned 16 years old.

---

**RECIPE**

### High Bush Cranberry Jelly

Pick berries when they are brown in colour, before ripening. Wash, and place in boiling water. Then strain the liquid through two thicknesses of cheesecloth. Take pulp and put back on stove to boil, adding sugar and a bottle of Certo. Let boil slowly until sugar has dissolved. Then pour into sterilized jars and seal tight. Makes a lovely tasting jelly eaten with cream.
*From Verna E. Bellerose*

# HOW A SETTLER CAME TO HAVE A HOUSE

Logging permits in the settlement were issued that set a limit at 50,000 feet of lumber per married person and 30,000 feet for a single person. This lumber was used for making houses as well as selling on the market.

The first standard house was built by Maurice L'Hirondelle in 1959.

Maurice made the necessary arrangements so he could build himself a home, a plan he'd had for some time. Whenever he got a logging permit, he would dry pile the lumber and save it. He did this until he had enough lumber to build a house.

John Trumbley had a sawmill in the settlement, and sawed the lumber. Once the lumber was planed by Marian Cox, Maurice started building. He had help from Gerald Heffernan and Tony Laboucan, but most of the building was done by Maurice himself.

As for the other materials needed, like nails, shingles, doors, and windows, the Metis Development Branch provided these.

In 1959, Maurice L'Hirondelle's white house was the first standard home built in EPMS. Photo from *East Prairie Metis, 1939-1979*.

— CHAPTER 6 —

# SURVIVAL STRATEGIES

In earlier times, the Metis settlements did not have the amount of local control and initiative that developed later. They were forced to rely on the Metis Development Branch of the Alberta government to bring about certain improvements.

Louis Auger shared his thoughts on the financial situation: "The first grant we got from the Metis Branch for creating jobs was 600 dollars. The supervisor hired by the branch got some jobs going such as fencing, fixing roads, and painting. We earned 60 cents an hour for these jobs. Sometimes I went for jobs outside the colony. We were given tools and machinery to use for our farming needs. We were also given seed grain to plant in springtime, which we had to replace later from our crops."

For the most part, the people of the settlement had to take care of themselves and each other. Louis Auger continued: "The families of the colony helped each other with the farming, planting in the spring, and harvesting in the fall. All the farmers had an equal share of the help, regardless of how much crop they had."

Wild meat helped to keep families from starving. Said Louis Auger, "There were plenty of moose then. One time I killed seven moose. Riel Andrews and my brother Joseph Auger went to haul the meat. I gave most of the meat to my relatives. My mother, my wife, and the other women made dry meat to store, because there was no other means of storing meat in the summer then."

Lucille Auger tanned her own hides. She made moccasins and mukluks from the finished hides. She'd take these to Enilda or High Prairie and exchange her handiwork for food.

## Larry Big Charles: Following Our Culture

I was originally raised in Big Prairie. My dad got scrip land, after the Second World War. At the present time, I live in a log cabin. I have a couple of other buildings I built on my own. I have trapped every year since living on the settlement. I still trap today at 66 years of age.

I've been following our culture for the last 17 years, working as doorman for the sweats and gathering healing plants.

### THE IMPORTANCE OF THE LAND

The land played an important role in the life of the East Prairie settlers. Whether it was for farming, trapping, hunting, or logging, the land meant survival for all of the people.

Even in the early days, the use of the land was regulated. Settler Louis Auger explained, "As far as I can remember you had to improve the piece of land you were given – like clearing, breaking, and having a dwelling – before you could get a logger's permit or a trapper's license. The logging permits were limited to 50,000 feet of lumber for making our homes and also for making a living. We did a little trapping in the spring and in winter, but beaver was limited to five pelts only, and later on, to ten."

Early settler Leonard Bellerose's family moved to EPMS from Corke, north of St. Paul, Alberta. His parents, Charlie and Bernadette Bellerose, farmed. "There was nothing to do for a living so we farmed," recalled Leonard. "We raised cattle, and we had pigs and chickens. There was no logging yet or anything else out there."

Metis settlers like George Bellerose knew how to log, which included how to work with horses. Photo courtesy Dorothy Bellerose.

> **RECIPE**
>
> **Baking Bread in the Olden Days**
>
> A long time ago, when people made bread, they'd mix the bread dough the night before. In the morning, they'd make a big campfire outside. Then, when there were lots of hot coals, they'd put the bread dough in a pot, cover it, then put the pot of bread in the hot coals and cover it all around and on top of them. Takes about an hour to bake. *From Louis Auger*

## CATTLE KEPT THEM ALIVE

Before Henry Prince moved to the settlement, he came to the dances, and got to know the settlers. Charlie Bellerose wanted Henry to move to EPMS, so Henry went to see John Bellerose and Norbert Andrews, who were on the council at that time. As a result, the Prince family moved to East Prairie in 1949. He and his family came with a team of horses on a wagon trail around Sucker Creek. They had nothing but the clothes on their backs – no blankets, and no food.

While they built a log cabin, the Prince family lived in a tent near Norbert Andrews' place. In the spring, they moved in. The family couldn't get help because Henry wasn't a *bona fide* settler, and had no right to trap or hunt in the colony. He was kindly given one blanket from the Belleroses. To survive, Henry Prince wrote to the Peace River Health Unit to try to get help for food and clothing. He received a cheque for 300 dollars. Henry had 12 head of cattle, but he left them in Sucker Creek because he couldn't sell them. He also had about 12 horses. By the time the family moved into their log house, Henry had moved his cattle to the settlement. Henry Prince claimed that if it wasn't for his cattle, his family would have starved.

# WORKING LIVES OF THE EARLY SETTLERS

Maurice L'Hirondelle: "The first thing we did in the late part of 1941 was to start cutting and putting up hay for the winter. We put up some good hay, but some very poor hay also. We were still making hay after freezing in order to have enough hay for the winter for the cattle and horses. After we got the hay cut and organized, my dad took a place (site), and we built a house there. Around October, we started building Dad's house. We built a sod-roof house, a great big house. We had no glass for the windows so we used flour sacks instead. We had a sod roof. There was no flooring. Dad had to break his wagon box so we could cover up the root cellar at least. After we flattened it out, we put the wagon box over the cellar. It made a table so we could eat.

"When we began to plant grain, people started raising pigs, chickens, and cows. We also raised sheep. When I started raising sheep, I used to have a lot of problems with bears and coyotes. Once, when I went shopping in Enilda, I told this white man about my problem. He said, 'Get a goat. They are good at watching sheep. Bears and coyotes are scared of goats, and they won't get close to one. A goat will keep them away.' The man's goat had just gotten a kid, so I bought the kid from him, and brought it home with me. Sure enough, as the baby goat got bigger, he was a good sheep watcher. No bear or coyote bothered my sheep anymore. I raised my sheep in peace after that."

Maurice's wife, Marguerite, had a spinning wheel. When her husband sheared sheep in spring, she would spin the wool and then knit. She made enough yarn for their children to have socks, mitts, and sweaters. She also made woolen blankets.

# PLANTING GRAIN, RAISING ANIMALS, AND LOGGING

Early settlers who farmed and planted grain included Solomon Johnston, known as Bear, a soldier during the Second World War. Also farming were many other settlers. On one side of the East Prairie River, the list included a bachelor by the name of Christmas Andrews, as well as Roy Haggerty, also a soldier. Maurice L'Hirondelle's youngest brother, Roy L'Hirondelle, was also a soldier. Alex Patenaude Sr. had horses, pigs, and machinery to use for planting. Felix Bellerose, Eddie Bellerose, Maurice L'Hirondelle and another brother, also farmed. Farmers located across the river were Charlie Bellerose and his son, John Bellerose. Up the river was Solomon Auger Sr. and Louis, his older son. Louis Auger had a fair-sized field.

In 1958, Eddie L'Hirondelle and his family moved to East Prairie. The year before, he put in his first crop. He made some money milking his cows and shipping the cream to buyers, getting three or four dollars for a can of cream. Eddie also logged with Kenneth and Peter L'Hirondelle for at least three or four years before he finally quit. He had a plow and a tractor when he moved to East Prairie and some old machinery. He also had just bought a young colt.

Lawrence L'Hirondelle sitting on his horse-powered mower, typical of those used to cut hay in the early days. Photo from *East Prairie Metis, 1939-1979*.

# WHAT IF PEOPLE NEEDED A DOCTOR?

Leonard Bellerose remembered when there were only three families in East Prairie Metis Colony: "It was paradise. Nobody got sick; hardly anybody was ever seriously hurt. Harold Bellerose fell off his wagon and went under the wagon wheel at about one o'clock in the afternoon. My dad, Charlie, hooked up another team to bring Harold to the High Prairie Hospital. The wheel had cut him open, but he never hurt his head at all. Another time, when they were building the first house, Edgar Bellerose chopped his foot. Other than that, nothing seemed ever to happen."

Left to right: Bernadette Bellerose (wife of Charlie Bellerose) and Sophie L'Hirondelle (wife of Peter L'Hirondelle) at the annual picnic of 1956. Photo from *East Prairie Metis, 1939-1979*.

John Bellerose and his smiling wife, Verna, with their eight-month-old son, Art, in March of 1944. Photo from *East Prairie Metis, 1939-1979*.

When it came to babies being born (and there were many), Bernadette Bellerose was one of the women who did the doctoring. When Theresa Auger was having a baby, Bernadette was called for. Her sons, George and Leonard Bellerose, took their mother across the river to Theresa. "You couldn't see the banks of the river," Leonard said, "because the water was so high." The river was full of driftwood and they would have to stop the boat and wait for the driftwood to pass before they could go again. But all ended well.

Bernadette Bellerose always used "Indian medicine," observed Leonard. In that era, that's all there was: practical medicine made using plants and roots that could be gathered in the area. "That's how she cured the animals. She used it on people, too."

Getting to the doctor in High Prairie was often an almost impossible journey. In October 1957, John and Verna Bellerose took their sister-in-law Julianna Paul, and John's brother Leonard Bellerose to High Prairie by horses and wagon. Leonard had chopped his thumb and Julianna was pregnant and had an appointment with the doctor. It started to snow when they left. They made it to Norbert and Madeline Andrews' place, spent the night there, and left the next morning. They got stuck at the Blueberry Patch, in the bush by a mudhole. It's a good thing, John Bellerose recalled, that the weather wasn't too cold.

John found that he had forgotten his chain to pull them out of the mudhole. He rode his horse back to the MacLeod's place to borrow one. When he came back, he pulled the wagon out of the mud and they left again. By now, it was snowing more. The wagon wheels gathered so much snow that he would have to stop and knock off the snow with an axe. He got stuck again right up to the mid-axle of the wagon wheels. There was no way of budging the wagon out this time.

John and his wife, Verna, made a big fire. After having some tea and a little food to eat, and drying his socks, John rode down the hill about three miles (5 km) to Joe Big Charles' place, leading the other horse. John borrowed a buggy and went back and loaded their things from the stuck wagon. They left once more. All the while, the snow never let up.

They arrived in Enilda at 4 a.m. on Friday. John Bellerose had a shack there, and he built a fire. They had something to eat and slept for a while. The same day around noon, they caught a taxicab that was on the way to the High Prairie hospital with a passenger. "Otherwise I don't think we would have made it," John said, "as the highway was plugged. Cars and big trucks were in the ditches in the snow. Finally we got Leonard and Julianna to the hospital. Leonard got his thumb fixed up and we left Julianna in the hospital. Good thing, too, because she had a baby girl the next day at noon. When we left for home on Sunday morning, there was about three feet of snow."

— CHAPTER 7 —

# NATURE ALL AROUND US

Nature surrounds East Prairie Metis Settlement. Mixed forests of white spruce, black spruce, lodgepole pine, aspen, paper birch, and balsam poplar are found in upland areas. Lowland areas, often wetlands, usually contain black spruce and tamarack.

Alone in the midst of an area of forests, swamps, and later farm fields, the early settlers had to do everything for themselves. That included fighting fires.

Here are some of the memories of the earliest settlers.

**FIGHTING FIRES IN THE EARLY DAYS**

Gilbert Auger recalled, "When there were forest fires, we would firefight for nothing. You didn't get paid because you lived there. It was your land. When you were firefighting, you travelled on a wagon with Wayjax (water) packs on your back, and a shovel used for making trenches. They supplied the dry beans for our meals, and we also had bannock and lard. We had to save our land, no matter what we had to go through, even if we didn't get paid for the work done in the colony. Anyway, that's how the people used to be treated. They used to work, but they never got paid."

Louis Auger offered a slightly softer explanation: "For firefighting, we used to get bacon, beans, baking powder, and flour as payment from the Alberta Forestry rangers."

In the 1940s, Leonard Bellerose and Riel Andrews were in Grade 6 together, with Howard Travis as their teacher. Leonard recalls, "That's when a big forest fire came through Sunset House, and one of their houses burned. We were putting it out. We started across the muskeg, and ended up by the Augers. That was one of the biggest fires I ever saw in East Prairie. It burned half the sawmill. We got two or three days off from firefighting once, when Madeleine, my brother's wife, came to East Prairie. Then we had to go back firefighting."

## WILD ANIMALS WERE ALWAYS A THREAT

In the 1940s, wolves were a threat to the settler's livelihoods. A wolf killed one of Maurice L'Hirondelle's colts. Wolves got three or four of Lawrence L'Hirondelle's cattle. Wolves also got a lot of the Auger's horses.

Bears hung around the farm fields. One day, when Maurice L'Hirondelle was in his fields using a tractor and a grain binder, it came to his attention that about half an acre of oat heads were pulled right off. There remained only the straw. Maurice had big fields then, about ten acres of oats. That's when he discovered that oats were the favorite food of bears.

Maurice and the other workers went to investigate. They figured it couldn't have been a horse because there was flattened straw all over, looking like a bed.

Maurice was sure that it couldn't be anything but a bear. The workers kept going around the field, binding. When they reached the same spot again, there was the bear, standing in the middle of the field pulling at the oats and eating them. When the men got close to the bear, it would head for the bush. As soon as they were farther away, the bear would return and start eating again. Finally in the afternoon, the bear got used to the crew. He didn't take off for the bush when they came around, just made way for them to pass through.

The men finished cutting the field towards evening. The next morning Maurice walked towards the bushes. He figured the bear was probably hiding somewhere in there. He was shocked to see the bear hauling bundles of oats away! Believe it or not, the bear would take two bundles under each arm. Maurice went on working, stooking the grain. After all, he said, he had a .22 repeater with him in case of a bear attack. He finally reached the place where the bear had been eating but he didn't see him anywhere. Maurice surmised that the bear was probably watching him from the bush.

This is how the bear ruined a lot of Maurice's grain, by hauling it away.

Bears weren't the only problem. There were so many fleas in the early days of the settlement, said Maurice. "I used to hang my underwear out at night. In the morning while they were frozen, I used to go out and clean fleas off them. One time when I was cleaning them off, I counted 70 to 75 fleas. I'd haul them into the house, and throw the fleas in the stove and burn them."

# MOOSE ADVENTURES

Maurice L'Hirondelle remembered that the settlement area in 1941 was pretty well wild. There was no road, just a Forestry trail. The only way the settlers could rustle up a living was shooting squirrels, trapping weasels, snaring coyotes, and shooting a lot of moose and deer. Thankfully, "we had all the fat moose meat and deer meat we wanted to eat," Maurice said.

In 1963, young Gary L'Hirondelle proved that even children can shoot a moose, but it is not recommended. His father, Eddie L'Hirondelle, recalls that Gary saw a moose, went home and got the rifle, and shot it dead. They discovered that it was a cow moose with a young one. The family adopted the tiny calf, feeding him with a bottle. The moose was the family pet until it got quite big, escaped from the yard one day, and someone shot it.

Gary L'Hirondelle's brother Ronnie feeds their house pet, a young moose, which lived with the family for many months. Photo from *East Prairie Metis, 1939-1979*.

In the early 1960s, Greg Sawan recalled one moose adventure in particular. He recounted, "One fall, my wife Elsie and I went snaring rabbits. We made camp on an old bulldozer road. I had a bad cold and I was coughing a lot. I guess the moose heard me when I coughed and mistook me for a mate. Anyway, we heard it calling and getting louder as he came closer towards us. There was a bunch of young white poplar, about three or four inches across, in the direction he was coming. Before I could see him, I heard a bunch of cracking and twigs breaking. He was just behind those small poplars as he came real close. I was standing on the road, and my wife was right behind me. As the moose became visible, I took a shot at it three times in a row. It fell on the spot. When I turned around, I couldn't see my wife. Here she was, lying behind a big log, hiding. She poked her head out and said, 'Where is he?' Here my moose was already dead. I'm not sure if she was scared of it, or trying not to frighten it away. I still think she was scared although she said she wasn't."

### A MODERN-DAY BEAR ADVENTURE

In the fall of 2017, in the early hours of the morning, a bear climbed on the deck of Dorothy and George Bellerose's home.

George, just about ninety years old and wearing only his shorts, grabbed his gun and ran out to scare the bear away. His gun wouldn't go off. The bear jumped over the railing and took off running, crashing his way through a metal fence and making a big hole in it. "Maybe he had a reason to live," George said, as he watched the bear go.

**2018 METIS MEMORIES**

## Marcel Auger: We Had Good Friends

We lived in Salt Prairie. My dad, Solomon Auger, had a homestead there. We had a nice log house, and everything was going alright. But the soil wasn't great, with lots of rocks and white clay. When Uncle Peter Tompkins told my dad about East Prairie Colony (it was called a colony back then), he said that a person could hunt year round. He also said that if you were a member, you could also trap inside the colony.

I was five years old when we moved to East Prairie Colony. It was rough living for a while but we had good friends, the Belleroses.

They helped us lots. Mrs. Bernadette Bellerose saved my life. When I was seven or eight, I had a nose bleed for a couple of days. Someone went and got her. She did what she had to do. She knew how to stop blood. She helped people with herbs. She knew lots about how to cure people. I still thank her for what she did for me. She was a good person.

Marcel Auger and Florence Beaudry enjoying life together, back in his community of East Prairie in 1984. Photo courtesy Florence Beaudry.

I didn't have much schooling. We walked two miles (3.2 km) to the first school. That was in the winter, when you could cut across the river instead of going around to the footbridge. In the summer, we used the footbridge, a three-mile hike (5 km). It wasn't easy for a 10-year-old to walk six miles (10 km) there and back in one day.

I did a lot of trapping, sleeping under spruce trees. When I was about 18, my brother, Gilbert Auger, and I went to Bellerose Lake to shoot beaver. We had to camp out. When I went to sleep, I covered myself nicely. The next morning, when I uncovered myself, the snow fell on my face from a spruce bough. It had snowed in the middle of the night. That's one way to wake up quickly!

I was 15 when I started working in the sawmill. If I remember right, I was getting 75 cents an hour. I started to run chainsaws. I worked wherever I could find work, and did any kind of work available. When I was in British Columbia, I was falling trees and doing other labour jobs.

When I started working for Buchanan Lumber in High Prairie in my early thirties, I did labour work. One morning, my foreman, Fred Olansky, asked me to run a loader in the yard. I didn't want to. He said, "Don't worry about it, just run it."

That was my last day of labour work. After that, I was a heavy equipment operator.

We did what we had to do. If you have to do something, my advice is do it now, instead of waiting around.

I did all kinds of work, working in the sawmill, running heavy equipment, road work, building up leases in the oil fields, running cats of all sizes, buggies, and graders. I worked in Beaufort Sea building a man-made island.

In 1984, I decided to move back home. East Prairie has always been my home. My partner, Florence Beaudry, worked for the settlement as a bookkeeper for almost 23 years.

Marcel Auger (left) with long-time friend and Cree author Larry Loyie, next to Marcel's water truck in 1998. Photo courtesy Constance Brissenden.

I worked for Dennis Cox (roadbuilding and leases) for four years, and Bissell's Lumber Mill for five years. I started my own business in 1994. I got a water truck, but someone else had also purchased a water truck. There wasn't enough work to go around in the settlement. I sold my water truck and bought a log truck, a button top loader. I did okay. I hauled logs to Tolko for seven years, from East Prairie to Grande Prairie, all over in the Peace Country. In the summer, I hauled gravel.

I'm retired now, for the past ten years. I do some trapping just to get me motivated. The reasons I'm trapping are because I enjoy being outdoors, I make extra money, get good exercise, and I enjoy being on a trapline. Even though I don't have to do it, I do it for my health.

We have many different kinds of fur-bearing animals in our area. We have weasels, lynx, marten, fisher, wolves, coyotes, fox, grizzlies, and cougars. Northern Alberta can still say that there are still wild animals here.

— CHAPTER 8 —

# BUILDING THE FIRST SCHOOL

A great example of the Metis spirit of determination is the building of the first school in East Prairie. The schoolhouse and the teacherage, where the teacher lived, were built in the year 1945.

Building the first school required immense commitment and great personal sacrifices on the part of the settlers. Many mentioned the first school in their life stories, recalling the difficult working conditions at that time.

Gilbert Auger recalled: "Pete Tompkins, the supervisor, used to come up here with the wagon and team. He hired me to work on the sawmill that was running so we could try to have a school. I worked for nothing; I don't know if anybody got paid. I was a tail-sawyer, and 12 years old by then. That summer when they started hauling the lumber to build the school, I worked on it again. After that I went to the school that I had helped to build. I was almost 14 years old then. I went to school for about a year, and that's all the schooling I got out of that place."

Built by the settlers, the first school opened in 1945. This sketch is by Alexandria Auger, a fifth generation descendant of early settlers Solomon and Lucille Auger. Alex attends the University of Alberta, and plans to take Indigenous studies. Artwork courtesy Alexandria Auger.

Gilbert had to throw over the slabs and hand the lumber over. Everyone took turns working at the sawmill because people were hungry most of the time. Nobody ever ate right, or had enough to eat. The men took turns working, sometimes for one day, or maybe two days.

Gilbert Auger continued: "The sawmill was run by a McCormick Tractor, with steel-spiked wheels. George Hopkins, a sawyer, wore a winter hat and a mackinaw, tied around his waist with a string because it had no buttons… but he did saw. Everything was used on that mill – a rake, used for haying, and small wheels from a mower. George Hopkins made that sawmill himself, using just about anything he could get hold of. After they had enough lumber to finish building the school, the mill was shut down and never used again. I never went to school either. After the school was completed, my younger brothers, Joseph and Marcel Auger did go there."

Felix Bellerose was a young boy at the time but he remembered the work clearly: "It was in 1944 that we started logging for a school in East Prairie, as there were no logs or anything. We decked the logs that spring, and then went out and worked on the road for about two weeks, putting in corduroys here and there, and fixing up crossings. Then we got George Hopkins in to saw our logs for us. George operated the first sawmill in East Prairie.

"We hauled his mill in with horses and his tractor. Sometimes we had to hook a team up in front of his tractor to get him through. The following spring we planed it, and I helped on that too. I was 13 years old by then. That summer when we started hauling the lumber to build the school, I worked on it again. After that, I went to school for about a year, and that's all the schooling I got out of that place."

The class of 1945 at the East Prairie School. Front row, left to right: Arthur Bellerose, Marina Auger, Joyce Longmore, Elaine L'Hirondelle, Larry Longmore, Richard L'Hirondelle. Back row, left to right: Gloria Longmore, Lorraine L'Hirondelle, Dave L'Hirondelle, Harold Bellerose, Don L'Hirondelle, Frank (Bolo) Auger, William Auger. Photo by Jack Kachuk, from *East Prairie Metis, 1939-1979*.

Maurice L'Hirondelle, father of 14 children, on building the first school: "I think it was in 1944 that we started fighting for a school and teachers. That was right off the bat, right after we got here, because I had children of school age and the Belleroses also had a lot of them.

"The public welfare decided to let us build a school. We decided to build a log school for ourselves, the Belleroses, L'Hirondelles, and Augers. We started sawing timber down and skidding them up, decking them up on a crib bank. We cut around 130 or perhaps 150 between us, including a new settler named Lawrence Renny. We got the logs piled, and wrote to the Metis Branch. We told them we had the logs ready to build the school. All we wanted from the government was the hardware, such as windows and nails. We didn't really ask for doors because we figured we could make a door. As long as we got the windows and roofing nails, we were going to build the school.

"The government realized we were determined people. They didn't like the idea of a log school, but promised that if we kept on logging, they would hire a portable sawmill to saw the logs. From there we could build a frame school. We told Peter Tompkins, the supervisor for the northern colonies, that we needed to be paid something to buy food. After that, I believe we got 15 cents for every log we cut. It was not enough. I think then they raised it to 25 cents a log."

The Metis Branch hired three carpenters from the outside to help build the school. Some of the local men were better at the job, recalled John Bellerose.

The Metis Development Branch would not pay the settlers for assisting in building the school. The settlers had to fight the supervisor in Edmonton, A. C. McCully, to furnish them food. Just food, never mind the wages, for the settlers to help build the school, said Maurice L'Hirondelle.

The money to pay the carpenters ran out. Only the shell was up and the roofing on, with windows, doors, and brick chimneys. Supervisor Peter Tompkins told the settlers, "It's up to you to put the siding on it, and put sheeting on the inside." The settlers worked all winter. In between times, of course, they went hunting moose and deer to keep their families fed. They didn't quite finish the schoolhouse that winter, forced to give up because it got too cold. In the following spring, after they got their crops in, they started to build again. The schoolhouse and teacherage were finished in time for school to start on September 1, 1945.

Maurice L'Hirondelle remembered the first winters in the new school, "The worst of it was that we didn't have anything to put between the walls for sealing the cold out. All we had was three ply of lumber, that's all there was, no filling of any kind. After the children just about froze to death a couple of winters, they decided to put shavings in between the walls, and shavings in the ceiling to keep it a little bit warmer."

Clarence Cunningham and Sophie L'Hirondelle marry in the old school, in the winter of 1958. Photo from *East Prairie Metis, 1939-1979*.

The first students in East Prairie were the children of Dolphus Andrews, Jimmy Longmore, the Belleroses, the Jackknifes, Maurice L'Hirondelle, and Roy L'Hirondelle.

The school at the time also served as a church and a community hall. Leonard Bellerose was married in the East Prairie school, as was Felix Bellerose, Don Haggerty, George Bellerose, and Clarence Cunningham.

## SCHOOL NUMBER TWO ARRIVES

Northland School Division ran the settlement school in the old schoolhouse. Then in 1962, the High Prairie School Division took over. They brought in a new schoolhouse which was placed across the road from Maurice L'Hirondelle's home.

Now there were two schools in operation. Children from Grade 1 to 5 attended the old school and the ones from Grade 6 to 8 attended the new school. When they passed their Grade 8, they had to either go to Grouard or to Edmonton to finish their education.

All this changed again when the gravel highway into EPMS was built. The children were bussed to High Prairie schools, starting in September 1967.

When the children went to school in High Prairie, the problem of lunches arose. Some families were unable to provide their children with adequate lunches. Community members began having meetings to discuss a school lunch program. Finally, in September 1975, the program began. Children were then able to take a nourishing lunch to school.

— CHAPTER 9 —

# MORE MEMORIES OF SETTLEMENT LIFE

## ...OF EARLY SCHOOL DAYS

East Prairie settlers were expected to contribute a levy towards the building of the school. Gilbert Auger brought up the rarely mentioned subject of a levy, introduced at some point after a supervisor began living on the settlement. "People used to take two wagon loads of wood to the school to pay their levy. Later on, they had to work for the supervisor for two days doing fencing, or work on parts for fences to pay their levy."

Jack Kachuk, the third supervisor and first teacher, was welcomed with open arms. On his harrowing first trip to East Prairie, Jack crossed the river

Teacher Jack Kachuk in front of the East Prairie school in 1946. Photo from *East Prairie Metis, 1939-1979*.

> "A few children spoke English, many did not…
> For many, it was their first school experience."
>
> – Jack Kachuk, the first teacher in East Prairie.

twice. Each time, the water threatened to float the horses, the covered wagon, and all its contents downstream. Jack arrived at the schoolhouse in the pitch dark, marvelling that he was still alive. In the schoolhouse, he found no bed, but a pile of shavings. He slept on the shavings.

Teaching at East Prairie was not a standard teaching assignment. In the settlement, the first job was to find the children and register them. The schoolhouse was not finished. For desks, benches and tables were built. The children sat at tables. A few children spoke English, many did not, having Cree as their first language. Some had gone to Mission schools, but for many it was their first school experience. Many were 14 or 15 years old, and still could not read or even write their names. However, Jack Kachuk reported that once they settled into the school they progressed rapidly. By Christmas of the first year, grades had been established.

### …OF HAVING FUN AND PLAYING GAMES

Memories of simpler times, even though life could be harsh and demanding, included happy experiences. Food was often scarce, but when it was bountiful, it was a pleasure. Social activities in the community included dances, horseback riding, swimming, annual picnics, and berry picking. Rodeos were held in later years.

Norbert Andrews and his wife Madeline at the annual picnic, June 24, 1948. Photo from *East Prairie Metis, 1939-1979*.

Dorothy Bellerose remembers one summer going out to Big Whitefish Lake. "I watched my *mosom*, my dad's dad, fishing in a small boat, way out on the lake, all by himself. I could hear him singing. He would bring home a bunch of eggs in a tub, and bring some ducks, too. The eggs he brought home were called *chakek* (mud hen) eggs in Cree. My dad and grandfather would go fishing. The bannock my mom made was so good. It wasn't fried; it was cooked in an open fire in a cast iron frying pan set on the hot coals. My *kokom* (grandmother) was a berry picker. She would go out and bring home some *sapominak* (gooseberries) as they were called in Cree. I never see these kinds of berries anymore. We would eat duck soup, bannock, and drink mint tea. Mmmm!"

One time, Gilbert Auger, brother of Margaret Supernault, bought a gramophone for 25 dollars. This was the year muskrat pelts were worth five dollars apiece. He also bought one record, and they played it over and over. Once there was going to be a dance at Charlie Bellerose's place, so someone came and borrowed the gramophone and the record for the dance. After that, Margaret Supernault's sister-in-law, Theresa Auger, ordered one record a month.

There was so little amusement in the settlement that Margaret would visit old bachelor George Harvey to read his collection of *Life* magazines. One time he complained because Margaret wouldn't talk to him, she was so busy reading.

Today, George Harvey's complaint would be that young people are too busy looking at their cell phones!

Children played games, one of which was called scrub. Leonard Bellerose recalled, "It was a ball game, with a catcher, a pitcher, and a first base man. There was always double scrub and there were always two batters. One would go up to bat, and he'd get to first base. He'd stay there. His partner would go up and hit the ball and he'd come home. That's how Harold Bellerose got his bad leg. Harold and Riel Andrews were both looking at the ball in the air and they collided. They both went down. Riel fell on Harold's leg and hurt it."

## THE LURE OF DANCES

Dances were always popular in the early years. Joe Patenaude went to dances, in and out of East Prairie, and was always the first one on the dance floor.

Joe moved into East Prairie in the summer of 1955, after a 500-mile (805 km) trip from Calgary. It took him 30 days, coming through the shortest way possible, which was through Valleyview. He brought 16 horses with him and came on a wagon team. His nephew, Ernest Patenaude, came with him; Ernest was on his way home from working on a sugarbeet farm in Lethbridge. Ernest chased the horses for Joe.

They didn't follow the highway because there was already quite a bit of traffic. As usual, the road from High Prairie to the settlement was in poor condition, but they made it. After some time in the settlement, Joe built a shack for himself. When winter came, the shack burned down, so he built another one. He stayed in that cabin for about 13 years living on the savings he had when he moved in. Joe always put in a potato garden to use the year-round. In 1971, Joe bought a house from Richard Patenaude. Joe now had electricity, a telephone, and two vehicles. He still had horses and he still put in a garden every year.

Maurice L'Hirondelle recalled, "I brought some music instruments with me, a violin and guitar, to the place where we lived together, in that big flat-roof house by the river. There used to be a dance every night, and we used to play for the young people."

Joe Patenaude arrived in 1955. He built a log cabin after his first shack burned down and lived there on his savings for thirteen years. In 1976, when this photo was taken, a prosperous-looking Joe owned two vehicles and his own home with electricity and a telephone. Photo from *East Prairie Metis, 1939-1979*.

Maria Auger and William Auger, in May of 1958, holding a violin and a guitar, all that was needed for a community dance. Photo courtesy Marcel Auger.

John Bellerose also had happy memories of dances in his family's house; "Sometimes there were two nights of dancing and my mother set a table until everyone had eaten. Sometimes the table was set six times before everyone had eaten. Everyone enjoyed themselves."

## NEW YEAR'S EVE FESTIVITIES

Eddie L'Hirondelle remembered the first time his family came to East Prairie. It was on New Year's Eve. "We went to Solomon Auger's place. There was dinner ready for those who wanted to eat, and whoever didn't want to eat, didn't have to eat. All the people got there and ate, and the women washed dishes after everyone was done. Someone said, 'Oh, we should have a little dance!' We said, 'Okay.' Only a few of the people were on the floor at first, then quite a few started. This was in the afternoon, about two or three o'clock. Solomon had this old barrel heater right in the middle of the floor. He said, 'Maybe we should move that stove out.' Everyone hauled the stove out.

"About four o'clock the next morning, Maurice L'Hirondelle looked at me. I was all played out by then, and he said, 'What do you think?' I said, 'I think I've just about had it.' Maurice replied, 'That's what I say too.' They were still dancing when I left. How long they kept going, I don't know. I used to come all the way out here just for that wonderful time on New Year's Eve. I never saw any fights at that time, so it was really fun."

**2018 METIS MEMORIES**

## Solomon R. Auger: A Grandson's Story

I want to share how we lived in the 1950s to mid-1960s in East Prairie Metis Settlement. I was there; I remember those days clearly.

My parents are the late Helen and Gilbert Auger. My paternal grandparents were Lucille (Lucy) and Solomon Auger and they are the ones who raised me. My grandmother said that I was 18 months old when I was given to them; this would be about June 1951. I was raised in East Prairie. My father, Gilbert, helped out when they built the first school here.

I first want to mention the veterans. My uncles and grandfathers were in the Canadian Armed Forces. My dad was also in the army. One of my grandfathers, Celestine Auger, aka Big Man, went to the First and Second World

Wars. When he came back, he started a farm four miles (6.4 km) north of High Prairie, Alberta. He had a four-room house in the town. With what he had in those days, the 1950s or 1960s, he was a rich person.

My grandparents had a mixed-use farm. We lived in a log house. We had a road going through our barnyard. Log trucks would hit and kill our cows. The oil companies would go through our yard between the woodpile and the house, really close, about 20 feet (6 metres) in between. In later years, they bypassed our place and the barns. We used slough water and ice for our needs, no plumbing. Firewood heated our house.

My chore was counting the animals. We had 75 head of horses, 34 to 36 cows, 35 chickens, 10 pigs, and six geese. I would help when the cows were calving. Sometimes we pulled the calf out from the mother; some cows had problems calving. This is the kind of work we did in those days.

The Auger family were early settlers, arriving in the late 1930s. This family photo was taken in 1954. Left to right: Solomon Auger Sr., Gilbert Auger (back), Steve Auger (front), Solomon Sr.'s grandchildren Ester Auger (white skirt) and William Auger, Solomon Sr.'s daughter Maria Auger. The horse's name was Skevin. Photo courtesy Marcel Auger.

We used to round up the horses and my grandfather or uncles would rope one of them. My uncles used to train the horses to use as saddle horses. My grandfather used to castrate the studs, too. We milked the cows, morning and evening. We fed the pigs, chickens, cows, horses, geese, and so on.

My grandfather hayed for the animals, plowed for barley, and gardened. It was a lot of work in the summertime. He would hay up the river. They called the different haying fields by name: The Haying Field; Louie's Hayfield; Harvey's Hayfield, and so on. We had big gardens. We had a root cellar to preserve our vegetables. We picked potatoes, about six wagon boxes of potatoes. Most of the vegetables we planted were turnips, carrots, onions, and peas.

My grandfather and uncles would hunt moose. There were a lot of moose in those days. I remember my grandmother, Lucy, making dry meat. I would say it was about five or more moose at one time to make dry meat. Again, this was a lot of work.

How to dry meat? Dry willows are used to dry the meat. We hauled dry wood, made smudge, and hauled dry meat inside the house for the night. In the morning, we would put it back outside to smoke some more. It takes about four days to do the dry meat. Once done, people from Gift Lake, Grouard, my uncles, and aunts, would come and get the dry meat and potatoes. Not much was left for us after that.

Lucy was a midwife and would pick herbs. We would go in the bush to pick herbs and use tobacco for the offering. She carried a small axe for this. I still remember some herbs by the smell. In the summer, she picked and canned blueberries, raspberries, and high bush cranberries, as well as plums.

My youngest brother, Clifford Auger, was also raised by my grandparents, and we would both pick berries. We used 10 pound pails and picked blueberries, raspberries, and more. There used to be a lot of berries at that time. It would take me about 30 minutes to fill one pail. Grandmother would say, 'One more pail, and I will bake you guys a blueberry pie.' We would pick more berries, but still no pie.

She also made moose hides. She'd soak the hide in water and cut holes around the edges. She used rope to put the hide on the wooden frame. First she would take out the flesh, then dry it for a day or two. Once dry, she turned the hide over and scraped the hair off. She put animal brain on the open moose hide, all over as it lay flat. Then it was folded over until she made a square of it. After that, she put a weight on top of it for one week. Next, she would soak it again in water, then wring out the water from it.

We dried the hide by holding it at both ends and flapping it over the open fire. Once dried, it would be smoked in a tipi-like structure over an open fire, making more smoke then fire. Once the hide was done, my grandmother made mukluks, moccasins, and so on. I used to help her with this.

Every family had horses and wagon for transportation. We didn't go to town much, just once a month. We lived a traditional way of life. We used horses and wagon to travel to Enilda. It would take about two days one way. It was a rough bush road, with water and mud. In the winter, we used a sleigh and horses. It was cold in winter. When we were cold, we would walk to keep warm. I rode a horse; his name was Shorty, a white horse. When someone killed a moose, we would use horses to take the moose out of the bush.

Later on, about 1960, some families had old vehicles, such as a 1949 truck or car. No one had a new vehicle. There were no roads, just the Alberta Forestry roads. For farming, we had a tractor and other farm equipment.

I started school when I was nine years old. I only knew Cree, no English. If I talked Cree, other kids would tell the teachers and I would lose my lunch breaks and recess. The Cree language was not allowed in the school. My teachers were Zane Dedeluk; Mrs. Heffernan; Mrs. Robinson; Alvin Cyre; Dale Perry; Mr. Hemphill; and Mr. Clossey. Our supervisors in the colony (now called the settlement) were Mr. Heffernan; Zane Dedeluk; Mr. Dixon; and Wayne McCullough. We had no school buses in those days, so we walked, biked, or rode a horse to school.

When Joe Patenaude moved to East Prairie, he stored his belongings in our old house. He brought many horses and got land in *pakan waciy*, which means Nut Mountain in English because nuts grew there. Joe was a great storyteller and had good stories.

The Louis Savard family came to East Prairie and lived beside the Auger's place. They first lived in a tent. Then they moved to the McKinley area where old Louis Savard had land. They had a team of horses for transportation. They lived on wild food and had a garden, so they didn't really need much from the store. They had a hayfield for horses.

The Jimmy and Clara McGillis family came to East Prairie about the late 1950s, with three boys and two girls. They lived where George Harvey used to live up the river. They didn't have any horses at the time, but later they did. Jim had an old car but didn't use it much as the roads were bad with ruts. We lived close to where they lived.

Every September, the families would help each other harvesting. East Prairie Colony had a tractor and thrashing machine. Roy L'Hirondelle used to run the tractor and operate the thrashing machines. They harvested barley and wheat. They used a wagon with a rack and horses. At our farm, it took about three days to thrash. We had granaries for the barley, wheat, and oats. There were about five or more teams that helped to thrash.

We had a school, but not the best school. At least we can read and write. We had outdated books but we still learned something from them. I walked to school about three miles (5 km) one way in winter and summer. There was no road, just a trail. In winter, we walked in deep snow.

Our log house was used for dances. For other recreation, we skated in the slough or on the river in winter. We played hockey using willows for hockey sticks and a tin can for a puck. In summer, we would play scrub, like a slow pitch game but with only two batters. If one batter is out, the batter has to go in the field, and so on. We went horseback riding and hunting.

My grandfather listened to the Montreal Canadiens on the radio in French. The radio gave us news, music, and sports from the outside world.

In 1966, I left East Prairie to attend Alberta Vocational College in Grouard, for trades training. There I met Anne Marie Cardinal from Desmarais, Alberta. We married and have three children. We lived in High Prairie when I worked for Buchanan Lumber. My in-laws told me that the North American Stud Mill was opening in Wabasca, so we moved there until the mill shut down. In August 1973, we got a house through the Transitional Housing Program. Anne Marie worked for the Province of Alberta for 17 years when they were building houses on the Metis settlements and isolated communities. When we got the chance to buy our house in Slave Lake, we did, and still live there.

I went to NAIT for plumbing. Anne Marie started working for the Lesser Slave Lake Indian Regional Council and has been there for almost 24 years.

Our children have done well. Our oldest, Michael, got his degree through the University of Alberta. Our daughter Colleen has her degree in social work through the University of Calgary. Our youngest son, Stephen, has taken post-secondary courses.

We have four grandchildren, Alexandria, Aiden, Brandon, and Luke. Alexandria is at the University of Alberta and is an artist. The three boys are in public school in Edmonton.

In the early years, hard work, determination, and the ability to endure hardships was all that was required of settlers. Some only spoke Cree, and did not read or write. Today we need education to find jobs. Grade 12 isn't even enough. There are jobs for the younger generation but they need advanced education or training in the trades. Drinking and drugs are harmful and counter-productive. For those willing to persevere, the sky is the limit!

— CHAPTER 10 —

# TODAY AND TOMORROW

The early settlers of the 1940s and 1950s had dreams. One was to have a good road into the settlement. Some believed it would happen; others did not.

Early settler Leonard Bellerose remembered a time when several families were visiting at Maurice L'Hirondelle's home. His dad, Charlie Bellerose, and his mom, Bernadette, were there.

Charlie said to Maurice, "We're not far off from seeing cars raising dust."

Leonard went on to recall: "The old ladies got mad and called them crazy. They said, you'll never see the day when there are cars in this place because the roads are the way they are."

Many years later, Maurice L'Hirondelle said, "Those old men were right. We've got good roads, beautiful vehicles out here, a school out here, and a church out here. Everything you'd think could never happen. The women were mad at us all the time for bringing them out to East Prairie. They didn't like it out here, and they were crazy mad."

The good gravel highway did come in the late 1960s.

In the late 1970s, settlers were asked how things had changed since the early days on the settlement, mostly in terms of the human side of life.

Margaret Supernault, a settler's daughter, answered this way in the 1970s: "The first settlers were kind, thoughtful people. There was always a helping hand. Even if their neighbours lived five miles (8 km) away, they were still available for help, day or night. Even though the trail that we called a road was mostly impassable, we felt safe knowing there was always a helping hand available. I don't mean to say that we relied on each other for grub, but there were times when you just couldn't make do. You had to borrow something like tea, flour, or sugar. All this was returned in due time. There was a closeness among the first families that you rarely see nowadays.

"Neighbours were a part of your everyday life. Even recreation was getting together with neighbours to go picking berries and have a picnic, or playing bingo at each other's home.

In 1956, a good road into the settlement was still a dream. Here, Maria Auger and Doris Auger Patenaude stand by a car of an earlier era. Photo courtesy Marcel Auger.

"The trip to Enilda, too, consisted of two or three wagons going together in case of wagons breaking down or the horses not able to make it.

"The most important thing on your shopping list had to be flour. During wartime, when tea and sugar were rationed, my dad used to pick red root, boil it, and mix it with a little tea. It sure tasted good. My dad told us it was good for back aches.

"I don't want this to sound like we love the hardships and struggles that we had. What I'm saying is that I wouldn't trade any physical comforts for the feeling of togetherness and belonging the people had in those days.

"Today there are good roads, children going to a good school, nurses, and a hospital a few minutes away, yet the people are not as friendly to each other. The friendship that was binding at the beginning is lost. Now people are trying to live as city people. They try to have more material things, to keep up with the Joneses, but they have lost one of the most important things, and that is friendship."

**2018 METIS MEMORIES**

## Eliza Big Charles: My Parents Taught Us How to Survive

I'll start with 1960, when I first moved to East Prairie. I was 11 years old, and moved with my parents from Atikameg. They were Elsie and Greg Sawan.

When we first got here, we lived in a tent for a month until my dad built a log cabin. We had our tent by the East Prairie River, with easy access to drinking water and also for us kids to have fun swimming and fishing. When we lived in the tent, everything we ate was cooked at an open fire.

We children would pick berries for our desert.

When my dad built the cabin he cut the trees himself, and hauled them with a team of horses. He filled in the holes between the logs with clay and moss so the cabin would be warm in the winter.

Our house was built across the river from where our tent was; the only access to cross the river was by a swinging bridge. It was called the footbridge, and held by heavy cables, with boards for the walkway. It was fun and scary at the same time to go across, especially when we had to walk across it in the winter time when we had to go to school. It was at least a mile and a half to the school along a bush road. Some children had to walk farther than that.

Elsie Sawan, in her seventies, in front of her racks for drying meat, sometime in the 1970s. She arrived with husband, Greg Sawan, in 1961 and raised eight of their twelve children in East Prairie. Photo courtesy Eliza (Sawan) Big Charles.

We grew up in the log cabin. Our parents taught us how to survive. They had a big garden. I learned how to snare rabbits, and shoot prairie chickens and ducks for food. Everything we had to eat we got from the bush. I picked berries and canned them, and made dry meat and smoked fish. As we got older and had our own families, we started our own gardens. Some years when we put in the garden, it was very productive. Other years, not so much.

My mom was good at making moose hide. I tried making moose hide one time with my husband, Larry Big Charles. It turned out pretty good for beginners. I even watched my

Frank Sawan, son of Greg and Elsie Sawan, plays a traditional painted hand drum in his sister Eliza's kitchen. Moose meat is drying overhead. Photo courtesy Eliza (Sawan) Big Charles.

mom do beadwork, which I tried. Later on, I did a bit of beadwork on my own. Recently, I started beadwork again to keep myself busy.

I still do some cooking outside every now and then. I make bannock with a cast iron frying pan. It still tastes as good as when my mom used to make it.

All that I have learned is pretty much from my parents. My mom taught us how to make a candle if you don't have power for lighting. You braid a cloth and soak it in oil, then light it up. She also knew how to make down-filled pillows and blankets. I did make some pillows but I haven't made a blanket yet.

In my adult years, I did mostly labour work, like carpentry, burning brush, and jobs with the Opportunity Corp. I went back to school when I was 48 years old. I graduated with my Grade 12 when I was 50 years old. It's never too late to learn. I continued doing carpentry and other labour jobs until my early sixties when I stopped working because of my health.

Now that I've been retired for a number of years, I still pick berries, can them, make dry meat, and put in a garden. I started growing roses. I also joined the Seniors & Elders Club that we started in East Prairie.

My house was built in 1994. It has three bedrooms and a full basement. I love it. I love this area. I have fresh air, trees around me all summer, and my neighbours are close enough but not too close. Deer and other animals come close to my place. Even cougars were seen close to my house a couple of times.

I'm 68 years old. I have five children, 15 grandchildren, and five great-grandchildren. What I learned from my parents, I hope my grandchildren will also learn and fall back on. Other than that, I'm pretty much staying close to home to enjoy my grandchildren and great-grandchildren. I hope I'll be around for some time yet to enjoy them and my life as it is today.

## POSITIVE CHANGES, FROM THE 1960S TO TODAY

Early settlers Louis Auger, Gilbert Auger, and Felix Bellerose wrote their accounts of some of the practical aspects of life in the early days. They stressed that people didn't have the sophisticated machinery available today, nor the efficient systems of transportation and communication that are taken for granted. Every job was demanding. Sometimes the only reward was the satisfaction of meeting a community need.

Many changes in recent years have helped to improve the lives of East Prairie Metis. Among the major changes in the 1960s were the opening of the gravel highway, completion of a steel bridge, the start of standard housing, the arrival of a church, and the power lines that ultimately provided electricity for all residents. More positive changes have followed, and are continuing to this day.

The highway (Range Road 161), a gravel road, was

started in 1967 but wasn't finished until the summer of 1968. The gravel highway solved the problem of the old, undependable wagon trails. The steel bridge was also started in 1967 and finished in 1968. This solved the difficult problem of crossing the East Prairie River.

In 1967, money also became available for the settlers to have standard housing. This was on a priority basis, as everyone badly needed proper housing. Most of the settlers had large families, and only log houses or small shacks to live in.

From 1969 to 1970, power was brought in. This was a fantastic change from the old, dim, coal oil lamps which barely lit the houses. Of course, after this, everyone had a television set.

When the power line was being brought into the settlement, work was done on an underground line for telephones to be installed in the homes. This was a terrific thing to have, especially for emergencies, as not everyone had a vehicle then. When someone got hurt or got sick, they could always phone a neighbour to take them to the hospital.

Due to the changes of the late 1960s and beyond, the living conditions and lifestyles of the settlers changed considerably. Most agree the changes have bettered the community. People have an easier life now than they had before but there is still much to be done.

# THE ARRIVAL OF A REAL CHURCH

Church was important to the Metis settlers. In the 1940s, the first missionary priests said Mass in their homes. After the school was built in 1945, it was used as church for a number of years. It wasn't until 1967 that a real church arrived by way of the improved gravel highway, from the Hamlet of Enilda, 20 km away. Members deeply appreciated having the Church of the Good Shepherd in the community. At the 40-year mark, in 1979, nine priests had come to the settlement to say Mass. One of these dedicated men was Father C. Knapen, who said Mass in East Prairie for more than 28 years. He served the community when the Church of the Good Shepherd was moved to EPMS.

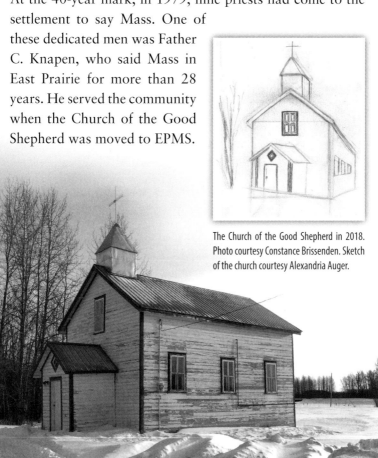

The Church of the Good Shepherd in 2018. Photo courtesy Constance Brissenden. Sketch of the church courtesy Alexandria Auger.

# EAST PRAIRIE COMMUNITY HALL: A WELCOME 1970S ADDITION

Bids for gravel were made on June 6, 1975. Soon after, work started on the EMPS Communiplex (community hall). Most of the building was done by the Opportunity Corp, formed in 1972 to create work in the settlement. Opportunity Corp work included a sawmill and logging operation, construction of the community hall, housing, land development, and clearing access roads.

Some of the lumber for the community hall was provided by the Opportunity Corp. This lumber was the settlement members' share. Some was from the Metis Development Branch of the government, which also provided other building materials.

The spacious community hall was completed in the winter of 1976. When it was finished, it had rooms on two floors. Upstairs includes a conference room and settlement office. Downstairs is a kitchen with two rooms for cooking and for

Aerial view, taken in the 1990s, of EPMS Communiplex (community hall), skating rink, and recreation centre. Photo courtesy Brian Supernault.

storing food. A hall with a large stage is used for traditional gatherings, dances, funerals, and other community activities. Smaller rooms include a utility room, activity room, and a booth for selling pop and chips during a dance or a bingo. The people of this community are proud to have this big and useful hall.

## THE BIG FLOOD OF 1996 LEADS TO GROWTH

Out of disaster, strength and growth are possible. The big flood of 1996 launched positive changes including a new bridge, paved road into the settlement, and upgrades to the water treatment plant.

Florence Beaudry recalls June 18, 1996, the day she was rescued by helicopter from what became East Prairie's biggest flood.

Florence knew the water was rising but she didn't think it was that bad, she recalls. Little did she know that the house she shares with Marcel Auger was completely surrounded by water. "I was alone in the house when I got a call that a helicopter was coming to take me to safety. I packed bags for myself and Marcel. The helicopter landed in the back yard to take me to the EPMS office. The wind was strong, and the helicopter was swaying. I thought Brian Supernault, who sat next to the pilot, was flying the helicopter. I told him, 'Brian, stop fooling around.' Then I realized he wasn't the pilot. It was a scary ride, even if it was just a short distance because it was my first time in a 'copter."

Brian Supernault, son of Margaret Supernault and William Patenaude, was on settlement council at the time of the big flood of 1996. Having worked for Alberta Forestry, he was aware how the weather worked, and how the East Prairie River worked. When it started raining in June, he kept his eye closely on the situation. "I told people to watch the weather," he recalls. "If there was going to be a flood, we would be in quite a predicament because of the old bridge built in 1967. We'd had prior floods which sent trees down the river, hitting and rocking the old bridge."

## VIEWS OF THE BIG FLOOD

Views of the big flood of 1996: The East Prairie River flooded its banks. Roads were closed. The land was saturated, as shown in this photo at the turnoff to Cattle Ranch Road East. George Bruneau stands on one of two bridges that crossed the river, surveying rising water carrying damaging debris. Photos courtesy Brian Supernault.

The rain continued. For the first time, the water went 10 feet (3.5 metres) over the old bridge deck. Flying over the settlement in a helicopter, Brian says the land looked like a huge lake. The old hamlet, including the graveyard, was underwater. Fortunately, the new town site, relocated in 1990, was alright.

Evacuations began and continued over two days. Families were pulled out, including many Elders. The helicopter even landed in two feet of water where it had risen up to front doors. Elder Harold Bellerose escaped to the helicopter by walking up to his waist in water.

"The pilot took big chances to rescue people," Brian Supernault recalls. "He should have got a medal for that flight." The rescuers used radios to communicate with one another and the settlement.

Some families stayed behind because their homes were on higher ground. But with power poles down, the power was out, and could not be repaired by ATCO until the flood subsided. The families cooked their food outdoors, just like in the old days.

The community was strong and worked together. As Brian observes: "It was such a difficult time, an emotional time for the settlement. But everyone was calm, and families pulled together. People were talking to one another. They helped each other like families are supposed to do."

East Prairie Metis Settlement needed help to move forward. Brian thanks then-MLA Pearl Calahasen for "twisting arms" to get a new bridge and a paved highway by 2006. When the Bakers Crossing Bridge (north bridge) burned down, the MLA lobbied for a replacement which was also built. The water treatment plant was also upgraded.

"We dreamed big," says Brian, noting the settlement's elk ranch, cattle ranch, and sawmill. "Not everything worked out, but we were moving forward."

# BUILDING A YOUTH CABIN

Just like the early settlers, young people worked with older EPMS members to build a youth cabin in 2001. Older members included Richard Supernault, Jessica Big Charles, Randal Sawan, Richard Patenaude, Wesley Patenaude, Robin Supernault, Jason Big Charles, and Roger Auger. The hardworking youth included Shaun Desjarlais, Heather Patenaude, Andrew Howse, Kyle Bellerose, Gilbert Hudson, Scott L'Hirondelle, Jarrod Cunningham, and Harlen Patenaude.

Elders and youth show their enthusiasm after building a log cabin in 2001. Far left: Randal Sawan. Left to right, back row: Gilbert Hudson, Kyle Bellerose. Middle row: Heather Patenaude, Raymond Supernault, Wesley Patenaude. Front row: Jessica Big Charles, Robin Supernault. Photo courtesy EPMS.

## COMMUNITY SUPPORT AND COOPERATION

The present holds modern benefits for East Prairie Metis Settlement members. The past, too, in spite of struggle, was good.

Many settlers remembered the early years as peaceful. Everyone was cooperative. If a person got sick, everybody would go down to help him or her. If a settler had chores to do, they did his chores. Leonard Bellerose recalled one example, when his Uncle Maurice was allergic to flour. Families went and helped him with his crop. People would sit up all night with a sick person. "In the old days, it was paradise," Leonard remembered.

In more modern times, the settlement continues to welcome newcomers. Myrna and Clarence Dumont married in 1964 and lived in Manitoba before moving to Calgary and Edmonton. For many years, they had a dream: to raise their eight children out of the big cities. In 1988, they applied for land in the East Prairie Metis Settlement. They were accepted and continue living happily in the house they built.

Looking to the future, Murielle L'Hirondelle, daughter of still-healthy settlers Dorothy and George Bellerose, expressed her deepest wish in 2018: "Our grandmothers and grandfathers survived many hardships. My hope for future generations is to be more educated so our community can prosper."

— CHAPTER 11 —

# ELDERS OF TODAY

## MEET MORE OF RECENT ELDERS

**RIEL ANDREWS** was born in Grouard, Alberta, to Norbert and Madeline (Willier) Andrews. His family lived in Enilda and moved to Sucker Creek in 1936. When the East Prairie Metis Settlement opened in 1939, Riel's father obtained land. The Andrews were one of the first Metis families to live here. In 1940, Riel's family moved to Gift Lake briefly but there was no school in the area so the family returned to East Prairie. At the age of 11, Riel started trapping, fishing, and hunting with Dennis, his younger brother. Riel had his own trapline in the Jerry Creek area for 14 years. In 1966, he went to work for Mannix Construction laying out culverts for roads. He worked for Mannix in Fort Simpson, the Northwest Territories, and Grande Cache, Alberta. He next worked for Alberta Forestry and was an Initial Attack Leader for 12 years. He then moved to Valleyview, Alberta, where he retired. Riel passed away peacefully in April 2018.

**JOSEPH AUGER** was born in Grouard, Alberta, to Solomon and Lucille (Andrews) Auger. Joseph moved to EPMS in 1942 when his parents obtained land. Joseph's parents taught him many traditional ways. His father, Solomon, was an avid hunter, fisherman, trapper, and farmer. Solomon passed his knowledge of the land on to Joseph at a young age. His mother, Lucille, taught him how and where to gather many different types of berries. Joseph spent the majority of his life in East Prairie, where he continued to hunt and gather berries, until his death in November 2016.

**LOUISE AUGER** was born in Marten River, Alberta, to Louie and Agatha (Houle) Savard. She had one brother, named Roy Savard. During her childhood, Louise learned traditional skills from her parents. She hunted, trapped, and gathered berries and roots. Louise also helped her mother tan hides for other people. At the age of 17, Louise moved to Slave Lake where she got a job working in a café. After two years, Louise decided to move to the East Prairie Metis Settlement where her parents had some land. Louise lived in the settlement and continued to hunt, trap, gather, and raise chickens until her death in February 2015.

**MARY AUGER** was born in Valleyview, Alberta, to George and Marie (Noskey) Badger, who lived in Sturgeon Heights at the time. At the age of two, Mary moved with her parents to Crooked Creek, Alberta, to go to school. The family then moved back to Sturgeon Heights, where they lived until 1984. The same year, Mary moved to the East Prairie Metis Settlement. She married Joseph Auger in 2002. Mary learned all the old traditional ways from her parents and continued practising them in EPMS. She also learned to play bingo, which she really enjoys. Mary helped raise several generations of children. She now lives in Sturgeon Lake Reserve near her relatives.

**WILLIAM AUGER** was born in Grouard, Alberta, to Louie and Theresa (Laboucan) Auger. As a child, William helped his father with hunting, trapping, and hauling the mail from Grouard to Atikameg twice a week using a team of horses. After his father came back from the Second World War, the family moved to the East Prairie Metis Settlement, where they had obtained land. William travelled back and forth from the settlement to his dad's trapline near Cranberry Lake. At age 15, William went to work on the pipeline and the railroad in Chetwynd, British Columbia, for one year. He returned home to the settlement, where he stayed until 1956. That year, he left to work with the carnival, running the Ferris wheel for one summer. In 1959, he met and became friends with legendary country singer George Jones. From 1990 to 2008, he worked for the City of Edmonton, visiting East Prairie on the weekends. His dad passed away in 1998; in 2000, William returned to East Prairie and moved on to his land. William lived in East Prairie until 2013 when he moved to Edmonton to be closer to his doctors.

**FLORENCE BEAUDRY** was born in Big Prairie, Alberta, to David and Madeline Chalifoux. In 1958, Florence left the Big Prairie area and moved to High Prairie to be on her own. In 1965, she moved to Edmonton, where she lived and worked while raising her five children. In 1984, Florence moved to East Prairie Metis Settlement. She worked in the finance department of the settlement office until she retired. Florence now has the time to crochet, knit, and visit relatives which she really enjoys. She is the longtime friend of Marcel Auger.

More memories: Hunters cross the East Prairie River with pack horses on the way to the Swan Hills, Alberta. Families would get together quite often to go hunting in the 1970s and 1980s. Photo courtesy Eliza Big Charles.

**ALBERT DESJARLAIS** was born at Forsythe Lake, Alberta, to Jim and Mary Louise (Trottier) Desjarlais. In 1939, at the age of seven years, he moved with his parents and siblings to the Elizabeth Metis Settlement, where he learned the traditional way of life. As a young man, Albert had to work away from Elizabeth, but continued hunting, logging, haying, and gathering medicines. In August 1969, Albert moved with his family to the East Prairie Metis Settlement and continued farming, hunting, fishing, and gathering. Over the years, Albert travelled to many parts of Canada and to New Zealand. He also visited the Peace River Corrections Facility to give spiritual advice to the inmates. He continues to help people in any way he can. He and his wife Alma raised eight children, and have always worked together.

**MARGARET DESJARLAIS** was born in the Elizabeth Metis settlement to Joseph and Maryann (John) Desjarlais. In 1968, Elizabeth moved to Edmonton to go to school. In 1969, her parents moved to East Prairie Metis Settlement, so she moved there, too. Margaret grew up gathering berries, roots, and other medicinal plants. She recalls everyone picking Seneca root to sell to a pharmaceutical company when she was a young girl. She continued to pick berries, to fish, and to hunt partridge and other small game. Margaret had three children, and has numerous grandchildren and great-grandchildren.

**MYRNA DUMONT** was born in St. Laurent, Manitoba, to Patrice and Marceline (Ducharme) Desjarlais. Myrna grew up fishing and gathering berries with her three brothers and three sisters in St. Laurent, which is on the east side of Lake Manitoba. In 1964, she married Clarence Dumont and started a family. In 1979, Myrna and Clarence moved to Calgary where her husband had work. They then moved to Edmonton, where they lived for five years, after which they returned to Calgary. In 1988, they decided they wanted to raise their five children out of the big cities. They applied for land in the East Prairie Metis Settlement, where they still make their home. Myrna enjoys berry picking and playing golf with her husband.

**ROBERT EMARD** was born in Heart River, Alberta. He was the only boy in a family with two sisters. Robert's early years were spent in the Kathleen, McLennan, and Kenji areas where he started trapping muskrat and squirrels. From there, he went to work in Chetwynd, BC, at a lumber mill. Over the years, Robert worked construction jobs, slashed for power lines, and logged. He owned a skidder and logged for Buchanan's Lumber in High Prairie, Alberta. When Robert wasn't logging, he was on his trapline or fishing. He enjoyed picking berries when he was hunting. He spent a number of years picking cones in the Swan Hills and Grande Prairie areas. He is now retired and enjoys life at his home in East Prairie.

**LOUIS HAGGERTY** was born in High Prairie, Alberta, to Roy and Ellen (Bellerose) Haggerty. His grandfather, James Julius Haggerty, had chosen Madeline Johnstone from the senior girls at St. Bernard Mission as a wife. They were married until James died at the age of 84 in 1943. As a young child, Louis remembers picking berries with his family. At the age of seven, he began helping out with farming chores. When he was 10 years old, and his sister Joan was 13, their mother passed away. They lived with their aunt, Sarah Big Charles, in Enilda. Although the children moved around many times from family to family, his Aunt Sarah was always the pinnacle of their lives. In 1968, Louis moved to East Prairie Metis Settlement and began logging. Throughout his life, he continued to hunt, fish, and gather across Alberta. At one time, he renovated an old granary of his dad's as a home. Interestingly, it had first been home to George and Dorothy Bellerose in 1957. In 1971, Louis went to Fort McMurray for upgrading, moving back to East Prairie in 1972. In 1974, he married Violet Cunningham and they had four children. Violet has worked for EPMS now for 29 years. In 1975, the couple lived in Loon Lake, operating the trading post owned by Frank Knibbs. After seven months, they moved back to East Prairie where Louis farmed and raised cattle, horses, and hogs. Louis has always been active in EPMS. He has served as a council member many times, beginning at the age of nineteen.

More memories: The Bakers Crossing Bridge burned down, leaving members with only one bridge out of the settlement for several years. Photo courtesy Brian Supernault.

**RICHARD L'HIRONDELLE** was born in Lac La Nonne, Alberta, to Maurice and Marguerite (Madjeau) L'Hirondelle. Richard is the third of 15 children. In the spring of 1942, Richard's family moved to the East Prairie Metis Settlement, where his parents had obtained land. Richard grew up in the settlement and developed a keen interest in politics following in Maurice L'Hirondelle's footsteps. Maurice was instrumental in the formative years of the Federation of the Metis Settlements, eventually as president of the federation. Richard served as chairman of EPMS at that time. Over the years, he worked both on and off the settlement in farming, logging, road construction, firefighting, school bus driving, and as an education technician. Upon his retirement in 2007, Richard settled down to enjoy his hobbies of gardening, volunteering, gathering, socializing, and travelling. In 2012, he married Pearl Banta.

More memories: Brian Supernault (left) and Jacob Howse (right) herd cattle at the EPMS cattle ranch. Photo courtesy Brian Supernault.

**FRED PATENAUDE** was born in Driftpile, Alberta. In 1959, he moved with his mother, Margaret Nohat Thunder, to East Prairie Metis Settlement. His step-father, Charles Patenaude, had land in the settlement. Over the years, Fred would go back and forth between East Prairie and his grandparents' home in Driftpile. Fred recalls hunting, trapping, fishing, and picking berries all over the settlement, and especially in the McKinley Creek area, where his family would go with horses. Other families would be in the area, camping and picking berries while the men hunted. From eleven years old onward, Fred hunted, trapped beaver and muskrat, and snared squirrels and weasels. He loved this way of life and continued with it until he started working as an adult. In 1975, Fred moved to Edmonton for work. He also held jobs in logging and oilfield work in Lethbridge, Cold Lake, Bonnyville, and Fort McMurray. Today Fred is retired and lives in High Prairie where he enjoys family life with his children, grandchildren, and great-grandchildren.

**ROSE (CHALIFOUX) PRINZ** was born in Edmonton, Alberta. She was raised by her grandmother in Joussard until she was 18 years of age. Rose recalls going to Virginia Hills, Swan Hills, and Kelly Lake every summer to pick berries and medicinal plants. She started hunting at the age of 11 with her uncles in the Joussard area and the "back country." In 1970, Rose married Victor Prinz and moved to East Prairie, where she raised her four children. She worked with her husband hunting, fishing, trapping, and gathering. Over the years, Rose worked hard and is now able to enjoy her grandchildren in the quiet way of life of East Prairie.

**DON SMITH** was born in Stoney Point, Alberta. He was raised by his grandparents, William and Sarah (Cardinal) Smith. At the age of 14, Don moved to East Prairie Metis Settlement with his sister Darlene to live with his mother and stepfather (Verna and John Bellerose) and his six other siblings. Over the next few years, Don found work in Stoney Point and Chinook Valley, and moved to Edmonton in 1962. Shortly after marrying Donna Quinlan, they moved back to the East Prairie Metis Settlement to raise their seven children. Once in East Prairie, Don farmed his land and drove the local school bus for many years. During those years he hunted and fished as often as he could.

More memories: Bridge repairs on the main bridge across the East Prairie River. Photo courtesy Brian Supernault.

**JOHN SUPERNAULT** was born in Grouard, Alberta, to Patrick and Margaret (Auger) Supernault. John's parents moved between Sucker Creek, Kathleen, and East Prairie Metis Settlement. His father obtained land in EPMS but died before he could build a house. The family had to stay in Sucker Creek, eventually moving to EPMS when they obtained an old log cabin as a home at the original townsite. Around 12 years of age, John started hunting, fishing, trapping, and picking berries with other families in the McKinley Creek, Hazelnut Hill, and Bellerose Hay Meadow areas. He continues doing these activities today. From 1974-1979, John worked for Social Services and Opportunity Corps in Peerless Lake, Graham Lake, and Calling Lake. Back in EPMS, he was the second manager for E. P. Wood Products, makers of tables, chairs, and cupboards. He then managed the Enilda store, and was a fur buyer. In 1983,

John worked for Alberta Forestry. In 1985, he was the first Aerial Observer with SRD in High Prairie. From 1987-1988, he worked for Settlement Investment Corporation as a loans officer, travelling to all eight settlements. In early 1989, he returned to EPMS to work at the store. Later in 1989, he became EPMS's public works manager. He also served on council for three years. John is now Wild Land Fire Fighter Coordinator and First Response for emergencies. John has three children, grandchildren, and great-grandchildren. He played fastball and slow pitch for the settlement's championship teams. His hobby is playing the guitar and performing.

**MARGARET SUPERNAULT** was born to Solomon and Lucy (Andrews) Auger in Grouard, Alberta. As a child, Margaret's family hunted, trapped, fish, and gathered berries and medicinal plants in the Whitefish Lake, Blue Ribbon Lake, Big Point, and Salt Prairie areas. She spent the years between 1935 and 1941 at the Mission in Grouard. From there, she moved to East Prairie to be with her family who were settlers. Margaret married Pat Supernault in 1943 and moved to Sucker Creek where she lived until 1948 when they moved to Kathleen, Alberta, to farm. In 1950, Margaret moved back to East Prairie and raised a family of 14 children while being active in her community. She continues to gather berries and enjoy life in East Prairie.

**MILDRED SUPERNAULT** was born in Tuliby Lake, Alberta, to Alexandre and Marie (Vivieres) Patenaude. In 1946, at the age of one, she moved with her family to East Prairie Metis Settlement where her parents obtained land. Mildred was taught the traditional way of life: hunting, fishing, trapping, gathering berries, and medicinal plants. As a foster home parent, Mildred raised more than 34 children over 36 years. She gave them a loving home, sharing Cree and Metis cultures, including survival camps, and hunting and gathering skills. The children learned ceremony, songs, and traditional dances, as well as crafts and beadwork for regalia. She received the 21st Annual Esquao Awards' Children's Future award for her work with children, as a mentor, and a role model of her East Prairie community and in her life.

# IN LOVING MEMORY

We remember East Prairie Metis Settlement members who have passed away since the forming of the settlement in 1939. We deeply apologize for any who have been missed and for any spelling or other errors that may be present in this list.

**A**
Garry (Slick) Anderson, James Andrews, Madeline Andrews (Sr.), Noel Andrews, Norbert Andrews, Randy (Sweet) Andrews, Riel Andrews, Blair Auger, Clayton Auger, Clyde Auger, Frank Auger, Gilbert (Mohawk) Auger, Helen Auger, Henry Auger, Joseph Auger, Louis Auger, Louise Auger, Lucille (Lucy) Auger, Maria Auger, Solomon Auger Sr., Steve Auger, Theresa Auger

**B**
Alfred (Casey) Beaudry, Yvette Bellam, Adelle Bellerose, Bernadette Bellerose, Charlie Bellerose, Darlene Smoke Bellerose, David Bellerose, Edgar Bellerose, Felix Bellerose, Leonard Bellerose, Madeline Bellerose, Marvin Bellerose, Oscar Bellerose, Verna Bellerose, Jack Big Charles, George Bruneau

## C

Candace Cardinal, Marlene Cardinal,
Ruby Cardinal (Davidson), Brian Chamberlain,
Joseph Courtepatte, Claudia Courtorielle, Beatrice Coutrie,
Bella Coutrie, William Coutrie, Darlene Cunningham,
Duane Cunningham, Marlene Cunningham,
Virginia Cunningham

## D

Dennis Desjarlais, Deom Desjarlais, Francis Desjarlais,
Gerald Desjarlais, John Desjarlais, Joseph (Joe) Desjarlais,
Ronnie Desjarlais, Sandra Desjarlais, Sarah Desjarlais,
Terrance Desjarlais

## E

Rowan Ellsworth, Edward (Lude) Emard, Joseph Emard,
Louise Emard

## G

Gertie Gauchier, William (Lover or Hollywood) Gladue,
Angelica Grier, Garret Grier

## H

Clifford Hackworth, Florence Hackworth, Ellen Haggerty,
Joseph Haggerty, Roy Haggerty, George Harvey,
Richard Holmes, Janet Hudson, William G. Hudson

## J

Marlene (Squally) John, Emma Johnson, Ernest Johnson

## L

Antoine (Tony) Laboucan Sr., Dennis Laboucan, Clara Leprete, Ida Laboucan, Joseph D. Laboucan, Joseph P. Laboucan, Louisa Laboucan, Louise Laboucan, Thomas (Tommy) Laboucan, Tony Laboucan Jr., Wilson George Laboucan, Alphonse L'Hirondelle, Celeste L'Hirondelle, Darlene L'Hirondelle, Dennis L'Hirondelle, Donald L'Hirondelle, Edward L'Hirondelle, Frankie (Bullose) L'Hirondelle, Gary L'Hirondelle, George L'Hirondelle, Gordon L'Hirondelle, Julia L'Hirondelle, Lawrence L'Hirondelle, Lorna L'Hirondelle, Lorraine L'Hirondelle, Marguerite (Margaret) L'Hirondelle, Maurice L'Hirondelle, Patrick L'Hirondelle, Peter L'Hirondelle, Ronnie L'Hirondelle, Roy Alfred L'Hirondelle, Roy M. L'Hirondelle, Shoreen L'Hirondelle, Sophie L'Hirondelle (Sr.), Tonnie L'Hirondelle, Violet L'Hirondelle, Adaline Longmore, Jimmy Longmore, Joe Longmore

## M

Victor McArthur, Claire (Clara) McGillis, Dennis McGillis, Edward James (Jimmy) McGillis, Leonard McGillis, William (Billy) McGillis, Brenda Moreside

## N

Hubert Nanemahoo

## P

Alexandre (Alex) Patenaude Sr., Alex (Red) Patenaude Jr., Charlie Patenaude, Charlotte Patenaude, Elmer (Fuddy) Patenaude, Ernest Patenaude, Floyd (Little Doug) Patenaude, Joe Patenaude, John Patenaude, Joseph (Joe/Rusty) Patenaude, Lana Patenaude, Lindin Patenaude, Margaret Patenaude, Marie (Betsy) Patenaude, Marie Viviere Patenaude, Rodney Patenaude, Ruben Patenaude, Wesley Patenaude, William Patenaude, Emilliene Payou, Patrick Payou, Pauline Payou, Peter Payou, Sanford Payou, Theresa Payou, Clarence Plante, Henry Prince, Victor W. Prinz, Yvonne Prinz

## R

John Richards

## S

Agatha Savard, Louie Savard, Louis Savard, Roy E. Savard, Roy Savard, Elise (Elsie) Sawan, Gregory Sawan, Henry Sawan, Jasmine Sawan, Klara Sawan, Randal Sawan, Donna Smith, Joan Haggerty Smith, Allan Supernault, Clarence (Manny) Supernault, Clayton Supernault, Donald Supernault, Patrick Supernault, Samantha Supernault

## W

Tonesha Walker, Hazel Whitehead, Millie Whitford, Caroline Willier